Target:
TRAFICANT

JAMES A. TRAFICANT, Jr. Born in Youngstown, Ohio, May 8, 1941; graduated from Cardinal Mooney High School, Youngstown, 1959; B.S., University of Pittsburgh, 1963; M.S., University of Pittsburgh, 1973; M.S., Youngstown State University, 1976; executive director, Mahoning County, Ohio, Drug Program, Inc., 1971-1981; sheriff, Mahoning County, Ohio, 1981-1985; elected to Congress as a Democrat in 1984 and re-elected every year up until 2002. In 2002, he was wrongfully convicted on corruption charges fabricated by elements in the Justice Department and then expelled from the House of Representatives on July 24, 2002. An unsuccessful candidate as an Independent for the 108th Congress in 2002. He began serving an eight-year federal prison sentence on July 30, 2002. His wife, Tish, and his two daughters patiently await his release from prison.

Target: TRAFICANT

The Outrageous Inside Story
of How the Justice Department,
the Israeli Lobby and the American Mass Media
Conspired to Set Up and Take Down
Congressman Jim Traficant

By Michael Collins Piper

AMERICAN FREE PRESS
WASHINGTON, D.C.

TARGET: TRAFICANT

ISBN: 978-0-9818086-1-1

Published by:

American Free Press
645 Pennsylvania Avenue, SE #100
Washington, DC 20003
Americanfreepress.net
1-888-699-6397
(202) 544-5977

To contact the author:

Michael Collins Piper
PO Box 15728
Washington, DC 20003
(202) 544-5977
Email: piperm2@lycos.com
See the website: michaelcollinspiper.com

ABOUT THE COVER: Congressman Jim Traficant, unlawfully targeted by the U.S. Justice Department, is shown in the foreground. To the rear is longtime Justice Department functionary, Michael Chertoff, who—as head of the Justice Department's criminal division during the George W. Bush administration—directed the prosecution of Congressman Traficant on trumped-up racketeering charges. Later, Chertoff was promoted to the post of Secretary of Homeland Security by President George W. Bush.

DEDICATION

To Jerome Brentar

One of the most gentle, kind, decent human beings
I've ever been privileged to know.

It was "Jerry" Brentar who first brought Jim Traficant's
attention to the plight of John Demjanjuk.

Working with Jerry, Congressman Traficant proved
Demjanjuk's innocence of war crimes charges
and saved Demjanuk's life.

To R. Budd Dwyer

He paid with his life for the crimes
of the Justice Department.

And to Jim Traficant,

The reasons for which you will understand,
once you have read this book.

Congressman Jim Traficant is shown meeting the press after being convicted on trumped-up federal racketeering charges in 2002. Despite facing a lengthy prison sentence, Traficant remained unbent and unbowed, continuing to proclaim his innocence, and, to this day, refuses either a pardon or a clemency of his prison term on the basis that, to do so, he would be required to admit his guilt and apologize for crimes he clearly did not commit.

As the evidence outlined in this volume demonstrates beyond any question, the judicial lynching of Congressman Jim Traficant by corrupt elements inside the U.S. Department of so-called Justice was, beyond any question, an outrageous—and perhaps the most blatant— politically-motivated frame-up ever to be documented in modern American history.

Even the vicious targeting of the late Pennsylvania State Treasurer Budd Dwyer (also described in these pages) virtually pales in comparison.

There is absolutely no doubt that Jim Traficant was thoroughly and completely innocent of the false charges upon which he was convicted and then sent to prison. Anyone who would say otherwise is either a liar or a fool.

Although Jim remains in prison and is likely to serve out his term, we can only hope that TARGET: TRAFICANT will serve as a warning to Americans of more of what they can expect in the days ahead unless they finally rise up and take hold of their government and bring the real criminals within to justice.

God bless Jim Traficant and all peoples everywhere who have felt the evil hand of tyranny.

—MICHAEL COLLINS PIPER

WRITE TO JIM:

James A. Traficant Jr.
Register Number 31213-060
Federal Medical Center
P.M.B. 4000
Rochester, MN 55903-4000

CANTEEN CONTRIBUTIONS
TO HELP JIM IN PRISON:

Federal Bureau of Prisons
James A. Traficant Jr.
Register Number 31213-060
P.O. Box 474701
Des Moines, IA 50947

(Note: please send only U.S. Postal Money
Orders in amounts no greater than $100)

HELP THE TRAFICANT FAMILY:

Mrs. Tish Traficant
429 N. Main Street
Poland, Ohio 44514

TABLE OF CONTENTS

Introduction
The "Crimes" Of Jim Traficant......................................11

Chapter One
Uncomfortable Questions...13

Chapter Two
Traficant and the Jews..16

Chapter Three
The Onslaught Begins...21

Chapter Four
The Set-Up...26

Chapter Five
False Charges...32

Chapter Six
The Sinclair "Kickback" Claim.....................................40

Chapter Seven
Tax Evasion & Racketeering—NOT............................44

Chapter Eight
Flashback: A Long-Term Vendetta...............................49

Chapter Nine
The Detore Affair...54

Chapter Ten
The Vote for Expulsion..58

Chapter Eleven
Traficant's Adieu..65

Chapter Twelve
Standing Up to the Judge.............................81

Chapter Thirteen
Traficant Speaks from Jail............................85

Chapter Fourteen
Rewarding the Real Criminals.....................93

Chapter Fifteen
Letter from a Political Prisoner....................98

Afterword
The Tip of the Iceberg 102

Appendix One:
A Voice for the People
Jim Traficant's One-Minute Speeches.........105

Appendix Two:
The Budd Dwyer Affair
A Retrospective..139

INTRODUCTION

The "Crimes" of Jim Traficant

Although there are probably dozens of members of Congress who could be indicted and convicted for major criminal offenses involving high-stakes bribery and influence peddling that is often quite open and never prosecuted, the Justice Department spent many years coming up with a handful of dubious charges against Rep. Jim Traficant.

Ask anyone who knows how it works in official Washington and they'll privately admit that the real reason Traficant was indicted on criminal charges was simply the fact that "the powers that be" didn't like Traficant: he was just too honest and too outspoken.

Right up front, let's lay it out. Here were some of Traficant's real "crimes" in the eyes of the elite who railroaded Jim Traficant into federal prison in 2002.

• Criticizing the Internal Revenue Service and calling for expanded protections for the rights of taxpayers under fire from the IRS;

• Taking a hard-line stand against NAFTA, the World Trade Organization, and so-called "free" trade and urging protectionist measures to preserve American jobs and defend domestic industry from predatory global speculators;

• Tackling not only corruption inside the FBI and the Justice Department, but also personally assailing the integrity of former Attorney General Janet Reno;

• Attacking Wall Street wheeling and dealing and raising questions about the enrichment of high-level financial interests through the lending practices of the World Bank and the International Monetary Fund.

• Accusing then-Vice President Al Gore of "trying to steal the election" in the midst of the long-and-drawn-out post-election debacle in 2000;

• Calling for the withdrawal of U.S. troops from trouble-spots around the globe and questioning constant U.S. meddling in the affairs of other nations;

• Charging American policy-makers with treason for having given top-secret U.S. defense and nuclear technology to the butchers in Peking;

• Coming to the defense of Ukraine-born Cleveland autoworker John Demjanjuk who was falsely charged by the Anti-Defamation League (ADL) and the Justice Department's Office of Special Investigations of being a "Nazi war criminal,"—only to be cleared, ironically, by an Israeli court.

(Ultimately, with Traficant sidelined in his own federal trial, they went after Demjanjuk again on "new" charges and restarted the process of seeking to deport the beleaguered old man. As this is written, Demjanjuk has been ordered to be deported; the final disposition of the aged man's case has yet to be determined.)

• Demanding that U.S. troops be sent to guard the Mexican border and prevent continuing hordes of illegal aliens—and potential terrorists—from entering into the United States; and—last but very far from least:

• Challenging one-sided U.S. aid and support for Israel, saying that the biased policy was to the detriment of America's security and Middle East interests.

Traficant was the only member of Congress—the day after the Sept. 11 tragedy—to point out that U.S. support for Israel and open borders were root problems leading to the tragedy.

While Traficant enunciated these truths, other members of Congress squirmed uneasily, sitting in silence, as Traficant spoke out—even in the face of his impending trial—never one to be cowed.

CHAPTER ONE

Uncomfortable Questions
From a Comfortable Man

Jim Traficant was elected to Congress in 1984 for the first time. He was the proverbial "man of the people." He had been sheriff of Mahoning County in Ohio and, at one point, many of his constituents, a lot of them steelworkers, were facing eviction because they were out of work and couldn't pay their rents and mortgages and Traficant, as sheriff, refused to evict them. And Traficant ended up in court and was sent to jail briefly for refusing to enforce the court-ordered evictions.

This is the kind of populist, a man of the people, Traficant really was, from the beginning. He had been a former drug counselor, very community-oriented. Earlier, he had been a popular football player at the University of Pittsburgh. Then when elected to Congress, he proved to continue to be very popular among his constituents.

Early on it became apparent that he was very different from most members of Congress. He began speaking out on a lot of issues that nobody—absolutely nobody—else would touch. He was very critical of the Internal Revenue Service and the FBI and the Justice Department. That was almost a guarantee of getting him in trouble.

There have been a lot of documented cases of the IRS and the FBI and the Justice Department targeting their critics and other people for political reasons. Democrats and Republicans—liberals and conservatives—have been targeted. Whole books have been written about this phenomenon. So here came no-nonsense Jim Traficant to Congress, standing up on the floor of the House of Representatives talking about these things.

Traficant was also raising questions about the fact—one that most people were ignoring—that the United States border with Mexico was virtually open, unguarded for all intents and purposes, the best efforts of the good people in the U.S. Border Patrol notwithstanding. He pointed out that we had troops all over the globe—in Korea, the Middle East, in Europe—policing the world, but illegal aliens were pouring across the Mexican border.

In those days—long before the 9-11 terrorist tragedy—Traficant was standing (virtually alone) talking about the possible dangers of terrorists crossing those unguarded borders. And what about those millions of illegal aliens who were coming into the country, consuming taxpayer resources? People criticized Traficant for daring to talk openly about all of this and more.

Traficant also dared to raise questions about all-out U.S. support for Israel at the expense of friendly relations with the oil-rich Arab states that were eager to have good relationships, politically and economically, with the United States. Traficant pointed out, and rightly so, that the United States was giving billions of dollars on an annual basis to Israel in the company of foreign policy measures that were inimical to the Arab world in general and most notably devastating to the Christian and Muslim Palestinians.

So this too created political problems for Traficant with the powerful Israeli lobby in Washington and with its various adjunct organizations in Traficant's home district and around the state of Ohio (where the Jewish community is particularly influential), not to mention across the United States as a whole.

On top of all this, the trade issue was a major concern for Traficant. He was concerned about the fact that a lot of the steelworkers in his district were losing their jobs as the steel mills in this country began relocating overseas.

Traficant was very critical of trade policies being carried out by both Democratic and Republican administrations. He was very critical of President Ronald Reagan for, as he put it, turning the United States over to Japan, and, of course, as soon as Reagan left office in 1989, he (Reagan) made a visit to Japan where he received millions of dollars in speaking fees from the Japanese, who said that he was the best American friend the Japanese ever had. So these trade policies that were harmful to American workers became a frequent target of Traficant's rhetoric.

Traficant's criticisms of the IRS led to his introduction of legislation to curtail IRS enforcement powers in order to give Americans more rights in their dealings with the IRS. He likewise worked to rein in the Justice Department and the FBI. He was very much concerned about the development of a federal police state apparatus in this country, a concern that is all the more notable because he was a career law enforcement man himself.

Traficant was raising a lot of uncomfortable questions about a lot of uncomfortable issues. And he was comfortable in doing would no other member of Congress would. In some respects, then, it was almost inevitable that the powers-that-be—particularly "certain" powers-that-be—would launch a drive to destroy Jim Traficant and put him in prison, putting an end to the career of an honest congressman whose only real "crime" was to speak the truth and to speak it loudly and proudly.

CHAPTER TWO

Traficant and the Jews

The blunt and simple title of this chapter—this particularly important chapter—will horrify many sensitive folks. But the bottom line is that, when all is said and done, it was the fact that the powerful Jewish organizations of the United States had decided Jim Traficant was "troublesome" that played a major part in the campaign to "get" Traficant. And *everyone* knows that to be true.

As an outspoken congressman who dared to raise questions about the one-sided U.S. "special relationship" with Israel, Traficant was already a target of the Jewish lobby.

However, at one point in his congressional career, Traficant got particularly involved in a controversy that was a major *cause celebre* for the Jewish community, and this was undoubtedly the proverbial straw that broke the camel's back: This was when Traficant came to the defense of a Cleveland autoworker named John Demjanjuk.

Certain American Jewish organizations (collaborating with the Soviet KGB at the time) had accused the Ukraine-born Demjanjuk of having been a concentration camp guard during World War II. Demjanjuk insisted that he was not the alleged "Ivan the Terrible" (as the concentration camp guard was supposedly known by the Jewish inmates) and thousands of people around the country rallied behind Demjanjuk, sending him money to support his defense.

However, until Jim Traficant came along, not one single member of Congress (including Demjanjuk's own congressman) would come to Demjanjuk's support, despite a considerable array of evidence that had been assembled to demonstrate that Demjanjuk was not "Ivan the Terrible."

So when Traficant came to recognize that Demjanjuk had been railroaded, stripped of his U.S. citizenship and deported to Israel for trial, Traficant used the powers at his disposal to investigate the Demjanjuk affair. Ultimately

Traficant was able to bring forth evidence that even the Israeli Supreme Court acknowledged was exculpatory and thereby set aside Demjanjuk's conviction and the sentence of death which had been levied upon the innocent man.

Thus, the Israeli authorities themselves had said that the American Jewish organizations and that the Soviet KGB were wrong. Yet, for daring to speak out on Demjanjuk's behalf, Traficant became the target of influential American Jewish organizations and their allies in the Justice Department's so-called "Nazi-hunting unit," the Office of Special Investigations (or OSI, for short).

It's not a coincidence that the very week Traficant was ultimately sentenced to jail, *The Cleveland Plain Dealer*'s Sunday magazine interviewed Eli Rosenbaum, the staff director of the OSI, who said, "There's only one member of Congress who has ever tried to take us on and interfere with our work and he will be sentenced in federal court."

In other words, the OSI and the Justice Department were crowing with delight at Traficant being sent to prison: they were saying, "If you take on the Justice Department, we'll get you."

And that's what Traficant contended had happened all along, after he had become aware that the Justice Department and its investigative arm, the FBI, had launched a wide-ranging investigation of which it was clear, from the beginning, that Traficant was the central target.

Traficant's brash public challenge to the power of the Israeli lobby was most certainly the primary reason why the Justice Department was so determined to silence Traficant.

The fact is that the Justice Department is known to be heavily penetrated in key posts by persons allied with a shadowy (but very real) clique that acts as an "inside" pressure group on behalf of the state of Israel.

In a series of exclusives in *The Spotlight* newspaper some years ago, the late Andrew St. George reported that within the Justice Department (and other federal agencies) there is an organized body of supporters of Israel who have formed a group known as "Nesher" (Hebrew for "eagle").

While Nesher acknowledged the views of its members influenced their policy decisions, the report by St. George was still controversial and one Nesher leader threatened to bring a libel suit. However, St. George deftly leaked the evidence he had to back up his story and Nesher preferred to avoid further controversy and no lawsuit materialized.

Not by coincidence, *The Spotlight* was shut down in 2001 by a federal judge, S. Martin Teel, who—prior to his judgeship—was a Justice Department attorney under the thumb of a key Nesher operative, Deputy Attorney General Arnold Burns.Along with others,Burns had been mired in an ugly scandal involving the theft by Justice Department officials of the INSLAW company's intelligence software (known as "Promis") that is used for surveillance purposes. The stolen software was channelled to Israeli intelligence, for whom Burns had done many "favors" over the years.

When the INSLAW scandal erupted and the owners of INSLAW brought a civil action against the Justice Department, the aforementioned Teel was the Justice Department's point man in the affair. He was later promoted to his judgeship after the sitting judge who had ruled against the Justice Department was deposed.

In fact, the aforementioned *Spotlight*—which was judicially eviscerated by Judge Teel in a thoroughly illegal ruling on June 27, 2001—had been covering the INSLAW affair even as the mainstream media in America was delicately and deliberately ignoring this Israeli-connected scandal. So Teel's ruling was no more than a blatant political payback.

One detail about Nesher and INSLAW brings the matter of Traficant's prosecution full circle: it turns out that the Justice Department unit that stole the INSLAW software was the Office of Special Investigations—the Mossad-collaborating "Nazi hunting unit"—that Traficant exposed as a fraud in the John Demjanjuk case. And considering the fact that the late former Attorney General Elliot Richardson, INSLAW's attorney, once publicly charged that OSI housed a secret assassinations squad, Traficant is lucky he was not murdered, as many persons connected to INSLAW were.

And this element relating to the Justice Department's campaign against Jim Traficant cannot be underestimated: it unquestionably points back to the role of the Nesher nest of pro-Israel advocates inside the corridors of power who demanded that Jim Traficant be destroyed.

You see, while then-Attorney General John Ashcroft—a religiously-driven supporter of Israel—was the "big man" who headed the Justice Department, allowing the persecution (and prosecution and conviction) of Jim Traficant to continue to the bitter end, the real power-behind-the-scenes was Michael Chertoff, Assistant Attorney General in charge of the department's criminal division and now, of course, today, chief of Homeland Security in the Bush administration and one of Israel's most stalwart assets on U.S. soil.

It was Chertoff who—from Washington—supervised (and obviously approved and facilitated) the corrupt activities by the FBI and the Justie Department in the campaign against Traficant. Craig Morford—the assistant U.S. attorney in Ohio who was the primary on-scene figure coordinating the attack on Traficant reported directly to Chertoff.

Although not well-known at that time to the public-at-large, Traficant's tormenter-in-chief, Chertoff, was a familiar figure in the pro-Israel network in Washington and inside the Justice Department, ranging back to his days as an assistant attorney general in New York City.

Chertoff was yet another protégé of the tightly-knit circle surrounding the father-and-son team of Irving and William Kristol—the senior Kristol an "ex-Trotskyite" and known longtime CIA asset who was propelled into a "leadership" role in the modern "conservative" movement, bringing a raft of acolytes in his wake.

Chertoff was among the founders of an elite "neo-conservative" legal group known as the Federalist Society that was funded by well-heeled foundations in the Kristol sphere of influence—namely the Lynde and Harry Bradley Foundation (with which William Kristol has been closely associated) and the John M. Olin Foundation—known for their ties to hard-line hawkish elements in Israel and to U.S. defense manufacturers which profit immensely through the U.S. "special relationship" with Israel.

In fact, as early as Jan. 29, 1996, *The Weekly Standard*—a "neo-conservative" journal funded by pro-Israel billionaire Rupert Murdoch and edited by William Kristol—hyped Chertoff as an up-and-coming figure in Washington, a sign Chertoff was a fair-haired boy in the eyes of the powerful inter-related Rothschild and Bronfman families who are the primary sources of funding for the Murdoch media empire.

Chertoff was chief counsel to Senate Republicans who were ostensibly "investigating" the circumstances surrounding the Whitewater affair involving President Bill Clinton.

Others would note that the Senate Republicans—with Chertoff in command of their forces—failed to pursue allegations of secret deals between the Clinton administration and Israel's arms-trading partner, Red China, over the transfer of U.S. military technology to China.

Then, of course, as assistant attorney general, Chertoff also oversaw the Justice cover-up of the apprehension of known Israeli intelligence operatives who were engaged in multiple venues of suspicious activity in the months leading up to—and on the day of—the 9-11 terrorist tragedy.

And above all, he was the one who directed the political assassination and criminal railroading of Congressman Jim Traficant, precisely because Chertoff's pro-Israel clique had decided that Traficant quite simply had to go.

CHAPTER THREE

The Onslaught Begins;
And the Media Joins the Lynch Mob

Having taken on the Israeli lobby and its allies at high levels inside the Justice Department, Jim Traficant set in motion the forces that were determined to destroy him. And upon the advent of the public disclosure that the Justice Department had launched a heavy-handed investigation of the outspoken congressman, the media in Traficant's district—and nationally—took immense interest.

The New Republic featured a critical cover story on Traficant in which the magazine dredged up ancient stories about Traficant's alleged ties to organized crime. And it is important to recognize that *The New Republic* has long been one of the foremost literary advocates for Israel, an important media cog in the Israeli lobby machine, published (until recently) by one Martin Peretz.

The article in *The New Republic* frankly noted that there was indeed a major effort by the Justice Department to nail Traficant on some charge—any charge.

In the many months of the long and drawn out investigation, Traficant talked about what was happening in his district, as he became aware that many of his friends and associates were being brought in for questioning, and Traficant's critics accused him of promulgating "conspiracy theories," saying that he was trying to build a defense that he had been unlawfully and unfairly targeted and that he was trying to cover up for his crimes. That was not the case at all.

The Washington-based *American Free Press* pointed out that, as foreign terrorists were said to have been coming into the United States right under the eyes of the FBI and the Justice Department, those two agencies had between 60 and 90 lawyers and agents—or more—working to "get" Traficant. What these Justice Department lawyers and FBI

agents were doing during the four-year period that led up to
Traficant's trial in the spring of 2002 was scouring all over
Traficant's district in Youngstown trying to find anything
they could to put Traficant in jail.

What they did, essentially, was find people in the district
whom they believed were guilty of other crimes (such as
tax evasion, corruption charges, whatever they could find).
At that juncture, the FBI and the Justice Department would
take those people in and sit them down and say, "We've got
ya. What can you tell us about Jim Traficant? Did you ever
give him a bribe? Did he ever ask you for a bribe? Did he
ever do you a favor in return for a campaign contribution?"

So there was this gigantic, taxpayer-financed army of FBI
agents and Justice lawyers trying to find out everything they
could about Traficant.

Now Youngstown had a reputation for being a center of
organized crime. Traficant himself alleged on the floor of
Congress and in interviews that a faction of organized crime
actually controlled the local office of the FBI as well as
judges—local and federal—in the region. And that was a
provocative accusation in and of itself.

Thus it was—considering all of this effort by the federal
law enforcement apparatus—that they would inevitably be
able to find somebody somewhere who would be willing to
make an allegation about Traficant in return for getting off
the hook, in return for getting a reduced sentence, or some
other form of favorable treatment in order to escape pun-
ishment for their own crimes that had absolutely nothing to
do with their association with Traficant.

In other words, someone accused of income tax evasion
might be willing to plead guilty to the crime in return for
probation, rather than a jail term, for having said that they
had offered a bribe to Traficant and that he accepted it.

During this time, the media in Cleveland and in
Traficant's home town played up the idea that Traficant was

corrupt, working in concert with "the Mafia," constantly reiterating that Traficant was under investigation. And as a result of the media onslaught, everybody in the region knew about the investigation: businessmen, political figures, mobsters. Everybody was looking over their shoulders and saying, "I wonder if the FBI is going to come after me?" And that is exactly what did happen in many instances.

The FBI was approaching many, many people and what did happen—as could be expected—is that many people concocted lies (often under FBI and Justice Department tutelage) implicating Traficant. And this is what subsequently emerged during Traficant's own investigation of the intrigues of the FBI and the Justice Department.

When his case finally came to trial, the judge, Lesley Wells, frequently frustrated Traficant's efforts to bring this into the court before the hearing of the jury. In some instances, the judge actually barred defense witnesses that Traficant hoped to call. In other cases, the judge limited Traficant's questioning of witnesses called by the federal prosecutors in order to prevent all of the exculpatory facts from being brought to the jury.

In short, people were being told: "If you don't testify against Traficant, you'll be prosecuted for your own crimes and sent to jail." In some cases, these people—who were under the gun—simply made up things to satisfy the federal authorities. In other instances, there were those who had innocent dealings with Traficant that the Justice Department and the FBI twisted in such a fashion as to make those dealings appear to be criminal in nature.

Traficant himself announced early on that he fully expected to be indicted. He said, essentially, "I haven't committed any crimes, but when the Justice Department and the FBI target somebody, they can get an indictment."

The old saying, of course, is that a prosecutor can get a grand jury to indict a ham sandwhich. What people don't realize is that there is no defense mechanism in a grand jury proceeding. A grand jury is conducted entirely by the prosecutors who bring forth evidence against a targeted individual who does not have the right to present a defense.

An individual who has been targeted can be called in and questioned by the prosecutors, but his attorney cannot come in and present a defensive cross-examination. So after several years of work and thousands of man hours spent, not to mention millions of dollars, the Justice Department cobbled together a multi-count indictment of Traficant.

There were headlines all over the country: "Controversial Congressman Indicted." "Racketeering" "Bribery" "Corruption" "Income Tax Evasion." It sounded very sensational and most people's reaction was: "Oh, here's another crooked congressman." Even people who liked Traficant started to think that "Oh well, he is a good guy who did a lot of good things, but he must be guilty of something. Where's there's smoke, there must be fire."

And that's precisely what the Justice Department and the FBI and their allies in the mass media (not to mention the Israeli lobby, which has long been highly influential through its contacts in the media) wanted people to think.

However, for those who actually read the federal indictment and who were familiar with standard political corruption cases, any honest observer could only conclude that many of the charges were "trumped up," if only in the sense that the charges were penny–ante in nature, hardly the major "crimes" that the Justice Department and the media were attempting to portray.

Yet, even some Traficant supporters, in reviewing the indictment, believed—without having heard Traficant's defense, as of that point—that perhaps there may have been elements in the indictment that could result in a conviction. But that was before Traficant began responding publicly to the specific charges and outlining his defense.

And as noted, the indictment itself was only what was presented to the grand jury: there are no indications of the defendant's response to those charges. It is impossible to make a serious judgment of the nature of the charges until the defense is heard.

As such, as Traficant's supporters began to explore the case, in the wake of Traficant's public contradictions of the indictment—those contradictions that the media dared to publicize—there were those who soon realized that there was indeed much more to the case.

It was more than just the government having targeted someone for political reasons and then finding evidence of that person's corruption. Rather, it was a sordid case in which the government was actually creating the crimes.

In other words, it was not a situation where the Justice Department had simply coerced false testimony against Traficant by threatening to indict someone who was guilty of other crimes not even involving Traficant, but in at least some instances the prosecutors had actually induced people to engage in activity involving Traficant for the purpose of trying to set him up and catch him in a crime, hoping that Traficant would fall into the trap by engaging in criminal activity—which, in truth, he did not do.

So all of this, taken together, pointed toward the fact that the case was trumped up from the start.

CHAPTER FOUR

The Set-Up

In considering the Justice Department's effort to "get" Jim Traficant, bear in mind that there was a previous major congressional corruption inquiry remembered as the "Abscam" case. In the wake of that affair, several congressmen went to jail and/or were expelled from Congress after they took bribes or conspired to take bribes from FBI informants posing as Arab sheiks and Arab businessmen seeking favors from those congressional figures.

In the Abscam affair, the federal prosecutors actually caught those members of Congress on film, including one who was taped stuffing wads of cash into his pockets as he commented, more or less, "I don't know if I have enough space in here for all of this money." It was almost comic watching members of Congress taking all of this money from these FBI informants they thought were "rich Arabs."

Conversely, during the entire prosecution of Traficant, the federal authorities never produced one videotape of Traficant doing anything wrong.

They never produced one audio tape of Traficant saying anything that could be used against him in a criminal prosecution.

They never produced one telephone tap of Traficant that they could introduce as evidence against him.

And although Traficant said it time and again, most people who heard Traficant say it probably never completely understood the point that he was making, and it was this: "The government has more tape on me than NBC does."

What Traficant was saying was that he was absolutely certain—as anyone, including a former law enforcement officer like Traficant, who knew how the government's prosecutorial methods were conducted—that there definitely had been video and audio surveillance of Traficant during the time that he was being investigated.

His associates—who were being directed to set him up or otherwise testify against him—were wearing hidden wires at the direction of the FBI. Traficant's home and office phones were being wiretapped. He was being videotaped in the company of those who later testified against him.

But the problem, for the government, was that of these hundreds—perhaps thousands—of hours of audio and video tapes, none of them contained any evidence that Traficant had committed any of the crimes for which he was subsequently indicted.

And that's why no audio or video tapes were introduced during the trial.

And if anything is certain it is this: if there were any such tapes, the Justice Department would have introduced them. So, in the end, this was the first major racketeering case of any kind where the federal authorities did not introduce any audio or video evidence.

The government had an interesting excuse to explain why this was so. They said that they couldn't tape Traficant in one particular office because the air conditioner was too loud or that the ceiling lights made too much of a hum. They also claimed that they couldn't get federal witnesses to wear wires because Traficant was a "touchy-feely kind of guy" who liked to give people bear hugs.

However, as anyone with a modicum of knowledge of surveillance technology knows, there are methods of surveillance that do not require big, bulky recording devices, nor do they even require placement of old-fashioned "bugs" in telephones. The government doesn't need any of this.

So the bottom line is that the government wasn't able to get any audio or video evidence against Traficant precisely because he was not engaging in the criminal activity that they claimed.

Now as far as the other "evidence" that was submitted—thousands of documents, letters, other material—the truth is that Traficant's fingerprints were not on any of the documents that were submitted as evidence against him.

However, a large assembly of documents, purporting to be "evidence," would look impressive to a jury when a United States attorney would bring in hand-trucks full of documents and say, "Look at all of these documents. These documents convict Traficant." But the truth is that those documents didn't "prove" anything.

The biggest problem with the Traficant trial came at the very beginning when this multi-count indictment was outlined by the prosecutors, throwing around "hot" charges such as "racketeering," "bribery," "conspiracy," "tax evasion," etc. This set the stage for the general public perception that Traficant "must" have been guilty "of something." And it was all over the news in Ohio.

In particular, it was big news in Cleveland, where the *Plain Dealer* (owned by the Newhouse family, known for its patronage of pro-Israel organizations such as the Anti-Defamation League of B'nai B'rith) made much of the investigation of the populist congressman.

And this is an important point to consider: the federal government moved Traficant's trial out of his home district and into federal court in Cleveland, denying Traficant his Constitutional right to be heard by a jury of his peers, the people of his home district.

Why this is particularly egregious is that most of the crimes that Traficant supposedly committed were allegedly committed in his home district and that these crimes, if they had really happened, were effectively crimes against the people whom he had been elected to serve.

In a case such as this, it would be appropriate to try the defendant in the venue not only where the crimes were committed but also where many of the key witnesses actually lived and worked.

In this case, though, the trial was moved to Cleveland at

the government's motion with the affirmation of a federal judge. And it should be pointed out that Traficant protested, but his objections were overruled. And then, ultimately, Traficant's post-conviction appeal of this motion was subsequently rejected.

But the very fact that the trial was moved in the first place demonstrates precisely that the government was determined to deny Traficant even the chance of having a possibly sympathetic jury pool in a city where he still remained popular and where many people believed, as Traficant said, that he had been "set up" for the purpose of taking him down.

Instead, the trial ended up in Cleveland where the hostile Zionist-controlled *Plain Dealer* newspaper beat the drum against Traficant, poisoning the jury pool and providing biased, distorted and incomplete coverage of the trial, just as it had laid the groundwork, in the proceeding four years, for widespread doubt about Traficant's integrity, generated by stories about "corruption" and "racketeering" and "the Mafia," always connected to Traficant's name.

Although the Jewish community's longtime hostility to Traficant was an "open secret," the trial judge, Lesley Wells, refused to let the congressman question potential jurors about their connections to groups such as the ADL or about their views on issues related to Israel.

Confirming Traficant's concerns, even the Jewish Telegraph Agency reported candidly, on August 2 that "few in the Jewish community will shed any tears" with Traficant's conviction and noted that that Bonnie Deutsch Burdman, director of the Jewish Community Relations Council of the Youngstown Area Jewish Federation, said that Traficant's views on the Demjanjuk issue "and his other maverick stances, aliented Ohio Jewish voters."

Then there is the question as to why federal Judge Wells was even permitted to serve as the judge in the Traficant trial. This is remarkable, even shocking, in itself: Traficant's investigators discovered that the judge's husband was a prominent attorney in a large firm, one of whose attorneys that was actually representing John Cafaro, one of the chief accusers brought forth to testify against Traficant.

To repeat: this witness against Traficant—John Cafaro—was a businessman who had supposedly bribed Traficant and this witness was being represented by the law firm that employed the judge's husband.

Any other American who was on trial for shoplifting would say: "Well, I don't want that judge. Isn't there some bias there? Aren't judges supposed to be unbiased and not have any connection to either side in a case before that judge?"

Well, Traficant put in objections and asked Judge Wells to recuse herself but she refused to do it. That's wrong. That's bias. That's—in short—a set up. Anyone can see through that. On this basis alone, any honest citizen should have shouted to the rooftops that Traficant simply could not have a fair trial, even if he was guilty of the least of the charges leveled against him.

But those people who were hearing the sensational news reports and reading the wild headlines about "the Mafia" and Traficant were not hearing about the behind-the-scenes corruption by the FBI and the Justice Department and by the very judge that was assigned to preside over Traficant's trial.

So although Traficant asked the judge to recuse herself from the case, she refused to do it. That's bias. That's wrong. That's a frame-up. Any honest person can see that.

Let us be honest here: there was a dishonest judge in the Traficant trial and there was also a dishonest jury selection process, with a jury drawn from a jury pool in an area that was not only outside the jurisdiction where the jury should have been selected from in the first place, but also drawn from a locale in which the local media interests were outrageously hostile toward Traficant.

So the trial was stacked against Traficant from the start, not to mention the charges themselves.

And let it be said frankly: this has been par for the course for more than a few widely-publicized criminal corruption trials and other campaigns of harassment and torment conducted on American soil: the mass media, in conjunction with elements inside the FBI and the law enforcement community, have worked together—conspired together—to defame the names and reputations of those who have been targeted.

And on more than one occasion those individuals targeted have been targeted precisely because they had dared to cross the powerful Jewish community in America. It's a little-known fact that could fill an entire book, but that's another story—or series of stories—for another time. But in the case of Jim Traficant, that's clearly what happened.

CHAPTER FIVE

False Charges

Many of the charges against Traficant, as we've pointed out, were fabricated by the Justice Department after an exhaustive and thorough scouring of the Youngstown region by the FBI.

Let's look at one of the charges. On Traficant's final day in Congress, when members of Congress were ostensibly "debating" whether or not to expel Traficant from Congress (when it was clear that the decision to do so had already been made), there were members of Congress self-righteously rising on the floor of the House of Representatives declaring that they couldn't think of anything worse than a member of Congress forcing his staff to do personal chores for the congressman on government time. That was just so "shocking, shocking" and morally reprehensible.

Let's look at the reality behind that charge—and bear in mind that it was a criminal charge—against Traficant.

One a number of occasions—and one of those occasions was when Congress was out of session, by the way—Traficant had members of his staff come down to the old houseboat in the Washington harbor where Traficant lived and help him scrape old paint off the boat. Traficant and the staffers sat around drinking beer, enjoying the weather and the companionship.

However, under pressure from the government, one of those Traficant staff members came in and testified that, well, yes, he had worked on Traficant's boat and that he felt like he "had" to do it because he felt like he "might" lose his job if he didn't.

The allegation that Traficant might have somehow pressured his staff member to do work that he didn't want to do doesn't ring true with anyone who ever knew Traficant's relationship with congressional staff members—from the highest-ranking committee director to the most junior congressional page. Traficant was known as the "friendliest" member of Congress and was even commemorated as such in the authoritative *Almanac of American Politics.*

However, even Traficant himself was generous enough to say that he understood his former employee was under pressure from the federal prosecutors. But this was the nature of the "criminal" charges against Traficant: that he had asked congressional employees to help him scrape paint off his rickety houseboat.

And for the authorities to suggest that there is anything such as "government time" demonstrates how truly outrageous the charges against Traficant were: whatever one wants to say about Congress and its staff members and all of the "perks" that they receive, it is also true that both members of Congress and their staffs—when Congress is in session—are extensively engaged at all hours, beginning early in the morning until late at night.

So the standard "eight hour day" for a member of Congress and his or her staff isn't reflected in reality. Congress is not an assembly line. It is not as though Traficant pulled staff members from an assembly line and forced them to leave the "factory" to go work on his houseboat.

But the way the federal authorities played it—and the way the media publicized the charge—it appeared as though Traficant had truly been exploiting his employees in the most venal fashion. Nothing could be further from the truth.

Similar charges were made by the government against Traficant relating to his alleged abuse of the rights and responsibilities of employees in his Youngstown district office. In this instance, a number of employees from that office came out to help Traficant do work on Traficant's father's farm.

Now—for a moment—ponder what we're actually discussing here: that is, we have a member of the United States Congress (a member of a very privileged class here in

America) helping do chores on his aged father's farm. You don't find many members of Congress doing something like that, and this says a lot of about Jim Traficant, illustrating that he is not your average member of Congress. Hard labor and Jim Traficant are not strangers.

In any case, there were members of Traficant's office staff who came out to the farm to work with the congressman doing farm chores.

One of those employees even said it was like a "health spa" for him to be able to engage in the physical labor, and he also liked to spend time with Traficant who is—as many, many people have said—a "fun" guy to be around, which he is. And friends do help friends do work.

But this was another of the "corruption" charges against Traficant: that he had congressional office staffers helping him out on the farm.

Bear in mind that President George W. Bush is known to take members of his White House staff down to his own ranch in Texas and those staffers have been photographed helping the president clear bushes and cut down trees and engage in the same kind of work that Traficant's staffers were helping their employer do on the Traficant farm.

The president, it is said, talks "shop" with his employees on the Bush ranch, and it is hardly out of the realm of speculation to suggest that Traficant and his congressional staffers spent time on the Traficant farm, while doing chores, talking about public issues. It is known that Traficant is able to talk about political issues and operate a "weed-whacker" at the same time.

However, Jim Traficant is now in jail for committing the same "crime" that the president of the United States has clearly committed, under the same circumstances.

One of what might be described as one of the "more serious" charges against Traficant—although all of the charges were serious, in that they were, of course, criminal allegations—was the claim by the federal government that Traficant was demanding money and favors from local businessmen in Ohio in return for providing them assistance through his congressional office. But as we shall see, the actual substance behind these allegations is rather contrived, at best.

Now bear in mind that Traficant's congressional district—through no fault of Traficant, by the way—had, at that time, one of the highest unemployment rates in the country. In fact, the high unemployment rate was precisely because of the so-called "free" trade policies that Traficant criticized so energetically.

But despite the economic devastation that wracked his district, one of the things that Traficant was most proud of, one of the things that he considered a great success of his congressional tenure—and he talked about it regularly, both privately and publicly—was the fact that he "brought home the bacon." He brought a lot of jobs and government grants into the district.

Although Traficant had a lot of fans nationwide for his outspoken positions on national and international issues, the bottom line of Traficant's congressional career, unknown to most people who admired him from afar, was that Traficant was very much community-oriented and deployed his congressional office as much as he could toward providing good, solid constituent services.

In one instance there was a construction company that employed roughly 75 to 100 people in Traficant's district and this company was having trouble getting federal government work contracts.

Traficant had known the owners of the company in question for years and they came to the congressman and said, "Jim, we'd like to get some government business here, doing some restoration work, but we're having some trouble. Can you help us out?" Traficant said, not surprisingly—

and as he should have, and as any congressman would have: "Absolutely. I know you. You're providing work for people here in the district. Let me help you out."

Traficant made some phone calls and wrote some letters on the company's behalf.

Now these people at the construction company were old friends and associates of Traficant and they had a family member who was in prison and they wanted the prisoner to be relocated to a prison closer to the family. So Traficant made some phone calls in that realm as well, saying, "Could you help these folks out? These are friends of mine. They're good people."

This point is important: these people were friends of Traficant's and he was doing things for his friends. However, this family had some legal problems of their own (that had nothing to do with Traficant) and the federal authorities found out that they had been having dealings with Traficant and the Justice Department told this family that they were going to have to help send Traficant to jail.

The government said, "What have you done to help Traficant? We know you're trading favors with Traficant. He's been helping out your company and your family member. He's using his influence as a congressman to get favorable treatment for your company and your family."

When push came to shove—and there was a lot of pushing and shoving by the FBI and the Justice Department—what happened was that somebody buckled and "confessed" that the company in question had poured some concrete on Traficant's father's farm.

That's right: the "bribe"—the "crime"—was pouring concrete on the Traficant farm. But the irony of the situation was that not only had the company failed to pour the concrete correctly, but they had also failed to pour the concrete where Traficant wanted it! What's more, it was left-over concrete from other company jobs that they couldn't use and needed to dispense with.

These were old friends of the congressman, old friends who employed quite a number of people in his district, and Traficant was doing things to help this company continue to be able to employ the people that it did employ. These were all the circumstances at work.

But by the time all of this made it into the federal indict-ment—courtesy of the FBI and the Justice Department—the pouring of the concrete was a "bribe."

This is one of the "crimes" of "bribery" that were bandied about in the mass media in reporting on the Traficant affair. This is one of the criminal charges levied against Jim Traficant and for which he was convicted and sentenced to a lengthy term in federal prison.

Another point in regard to this particular charge, a point that Traficant's federal accusers wanted to keep under wraps, is that the family that owned the construction com-pany which Traficant had helped out also owned a farm themselves, and that, for years, Traficant had been doing farm work on that other family's farm. That family owed Traficant money for the work he had performed.

Traficant—when not in Washington—had gone out to that other family's farm, using his own equipment, and had done work for them. However, they hadn't paid Traficant and when it came time that Traficant needed concrete poured on his farm, they were able to pay Traficant back, at least in part, by pouring that concrete.

So even this charge was not so cut-and-dried. It wasn't simply a situation of Traficant using his congressional influ-ence to do favors for this family in return for getting some free concrete (of all things).

It wasn't a case of a congressman doing sneaky favors at all and then getting a pay-off. The bigger picture—involving Traficant's long-standing personal business relationship with this family, involving the trade of concrete for farm work—was suppressed by the federal prosecutors.

But aside from even that, the very idea that Traficant was somehow guilty of a crime by having made efforts to get federal contracts for a business (employing so many of his constituents) stretches credulity when one realizes that— every day—members of Congress do favors for employers (big and small) in their own districts and that many of those employers regularly make campaign contributions to those members of Congress.

However, only when federal prosecutors "decide" that those contributions are "bribes"—as they did in the case of Jim Traficant whom they were clearly determined to "get"— does a criminal case emerge.

Confirming the long-standing charge by Traficant that the FBI and the Justice Department were determined to "get" him, a witness testifying on Traficant's behalf in his federal corruption trial in Cleveland told jurors that the FBI had falsely led her to believe that Traficant—her longtime friend and employer—was plotting to have her murdered.

The woman, Sandy Ferrante, who lived and worked on Traficant's family farm for 17 years, said that she was so frightened by the FBI's claim that she ended up testifying against the congressman before the grand jury that ultimately indicted him.

Miss Ferrante said the FBI played a tape for her in which another worker at the farm talked about a so-called murder plot, but that, in fact, Traficant's voice was not on the tape.

After that, she said, the FBI dramatically took her into protective custody, ostensibly to protect her from Traficant, whom she clearly needed no protection from.

Since that time, Miss Ferrante publicly apologized to Traficant for statements that she made about the case to the press and offered to testify at the trial on his behalf. She told the trial jury that "I felt used by the FBI," at the time she had been tricked into testifying before the grand jury that laid down the indictment against her friend, the congressman.

Although the FBI and the Justice Department cooked up quite a witch's brew of charges against the congressman, they never made a single attempt to charge him with plotting Miss Ferrante's murder, which suggests, of course, that no such murder plot was ever hatched but that,instead, the plot was a trick by the FBI to frighten Miss Ferrante into testifying against Traficant in the first place.

CHAPTER SIX

The Sinclair "Kickback" Claim:
Absolute Proof of a Government Frame-Up

Another of the highly touted "crimes" of Jim Traficant, as outlined in the federal indictment, was that he took a regular $2,500 kickback from the pay of one of his employees, R. Allen Sinclair.

It seems that for roughly a period of about a year, Sinclair would deposit into his bank account his government check from the federal payroll, as a congressional employee on the staff of Jim Traficant. From that bank account, Sinclair would then deduct $2,500 in cash.

At the direction of the federal prosecutors, Sinclair would later testify that he was giving that $2,500 in cash as a secret payment—a salary "kickback"—to Traficant. Sinclair asserted that Traficant had told him (Sinclair) that he would hire him in return for a regular kickback in that amount.

Now such a deal would constitute a crime. That kind of arrangement is not allowed. However, the members of the jury in the Traficant case were not allowed to hear critical evidence brought forth by an investigator for Traficant, a former Secret Service agent who specialized in financial crimes. The evidence withheld from the jury was this:

Mr. Sinclair did not just have one bank account (the one from which he took the regular $2,500 deduction that was supposedly given in cash to Traficant) but he had, in fact, at least five different bank accounts.

And every time Sinclair withdrew $2,500 in cash from the bank account where he deposited his Traficant payroll check, a corresponding $2,500 cash deposit was being made into another of Sinclair's bank accounts.

To repeat: What was really happening was that Sinclair was regularly taking $2,500 in cash out of his bank account where he deposited his congressional staff paycheck and putting this money in another of his personal bank accounts. In short, the money was NOT being used to pay a kickback to the congressman.

Initially, when first questioned by the FBI about his relationship with Traficant, as part of the Justice Department's broad-ranging campaign to "get" the populist congressman, Sinclair told the FBI that he knew of no criminal activity by Traficant and said that he would not be a part of any attempt to "get" Traficant.

However, when the FBI found evidence of a number of apparent ethical lapses by Sinclair—who was an attorney— he (Sinclair) was put under the gun and Sinclair suddenly became a federal witness against Traficant.

It can be speculated, with good reason, that the government, in fact, knew of Sinclair's problems and went to him and told him: "We understand you're going to work for Jim Traficant. From now on, you start taking $2,500 a month out of the bank account where you deposit your Traficant payroll check and put it somewhere else. When we need you, Sinclair, you'll testify that this was a kickback from you to Jim Traficant."

Sinclair later testified that he had this array of envelopes in which he gave the alleged regular $2,500 kickbacks to Traficant, but the FBI couldn't produce any of Traficant's fingerprints on these envelopes.

Finally, during the trial in which these allegations were made, when Traficant made the attempt to bring in his expert witness, his investigator, the former Secret Service agent, to testify regarding Sinclair's bank account legerdemain—the transfer of $2,500 in cash from one bank account to another—federal Judge Lesley Wells refused to allow Traficant to question his own expert witness before the jury. The jury never heard any of this evidence.

And this was considered one of the "big" charges against Traficant. Yet, he was not allowed to bring in an expert witness who could have derailed—or, at the very least, raised a reasonable doubt about—Sinclair's testimony while under the gun of the Justice Department, facing the possibility of losing his license to practice law and even going to jail.

And this is the one charge even Traficant's defenders thought—having heard the initial government claims—that perhaps Traficant might conceivably have been guilty of!

People knew the congressman was regularly being garnisheed by the IRS of a substantial portion of his congressional salary and some folks surmised perhaps Traficant had indeed worked out such an arrangement with Sinclair, but this was not the case at all.

In any event, the biased federal judge refused to let exculpatory evidence be heard in one of the key elements of the federal indictment.

And this was not the only instance in the Traficant trial where the judge frustrated Traficant's efforts to bring in defense witnesses or documenary evidence that would have substantially undermined what was actually a very flimsy case against Traficant cobbled together by the FBI and the Justice Department.

At times the judge would actually stop the proceedings, order the jury out of the courtroom, and then say, "All right, Mr. Traficant, let me hear what you want to present," and then after Traficant presented his evidence, she would say, "I won't allow that entered into the record before the jury" (or words to that effect).

Then the jury would be brought back into the courtroom. The jury would never be permitted to hear tape recordings or paperwork or witnesses that Traficant wanted to introduce in his own defense. So the jury never actually heard Traficant's substantial defenses against many of the federal charges against him.

That's the American "justice" system as it worked—or didn't work—in the Traficant case.

Thus, in the instance of the Sinclair testimony, the circumstances indicate that the federal prosecutors actually "set up"Traficant, rather than manipulated a pre-existing set of circumstnces.

This was not an instance where the government discovered the existence of the fact that Sinclair was regularly deducting $2,500 from one bank account (in cash) and depositing it in another bank account and then, on this basis, conjured up the theory that this was a cash kickback to Traficant.

Rather, it is all too apparent that the government swooped down on Sinclair and holding the threat of prosecution against him for his own misdeeds, ordered Sinclair to begin to carry out the regular $2,500 cash transfer as a deliberately orchestrated scheme (under the government's direction) to frame Traficant.

The entire "kickback" scenario had been concocuted by the federal government, and the federal judge played her part in the effort to "get" Traficant by preventing Traficant from bringing in the evidence vital to his defense.

CHAPTER SEVEN

Tax Evasion & Racketeering—NOT!

Newspaper headlines and media sound bites played up the theme that Jim Traficant was charged with "tax evasion," and many hard-pressed American taxpayers are quick to denounce others (especially members of Congress) who are presumed (or charged outright) with having failed to pay their own taxes.

But the tax evasion charges against Traficant were founded on the theory that Traficant failed to pay taxes, for example, on the kickbacks that he was alleged to have received from Sinclair. However—as we have seen—Traficant never actually received those kickbacks in the first place, so Traficant could hardly have been responsible for paying taxes on "income" that he never received, whether that income was legal, or, in this instance, illegal.

The government also contended that Traficant owed income taxes on the alleged favors such as the pouring of the concrete on his father's farm (which the government contended constituted a form of "income"), even though, of course, the pouring of the concrete was a return favor for the work Traficant had done—unpaid work—on the farm owned by the family that had poured the concrete on the Traficant farm.

The government prosecutors also contended that because some local businessmen had made campaign contributions—totally legally contributions—to Traficant, during which time Traficant had been working to steer government contracts to those businesses (which employed many people in his home district), those contributions were actually "bribes," not campaign contributions.

Therefore, in the government's thoroughly concocted case, Traficant owed taxes on those alleged "bribes" (which were not bribes at all).

We also heard, regularly and loudly, in the mainstream

media, that Traficant was guilty of "racketeering." When hearing the term "racketeering," the average American thinks of mobsters and organized crime, something out of Hollywood's *Godfather* series or, more recently, the popular *Sopranos* television show.

The average American has no understanding of what the term "racketeering" really means in the legal parlance in which it was used in the Traficant affair.

The term "racketeering" is a legal term that can be construed to mean any continuing pattern of criminal activity. So the "racketeering" charge against Traficant did not involve Traficant running a house of prostitution or engaging in an illegal gambling enterprise or distributing drugs or money laundering or bootlegging video cassettes.

Instead, what the government prosecutors were alleging was that by supposedly continually committing "crimes" (of the type of non-crimes that we've already examined) by using the power and mechanism of his congressional office to commit such crimes that this, in itself, was "racketeering" and that Traficant had converted his congressional office itself into a "racketeering enterprise."

However, the whole alleged "pattern" was no pattern at all, since none of the charges against Traficant was legitimate in the first place and his actions were regular and thoroughly proper constituent services of the type that all members of Congress carry out in the normal course of providing services and assistance to their constituents, both individuals and businesses of a wide variety.

There was no tax evasion.

There were no bribes.

There were no illegal favors.

The term—and the charge—of "racketeering" was fancy window dressing, the icing on the cake, colorful packaging for a totally fraudulent assembly of false, conjured and trumped-up charges.

The government doesn't satisfy itself—when going all out to "get" a controversial (and popular) public figure such as Traficant, a long-time target of the ire of powerful private special interest groups and foreign lobbies—by simply laying out charges such as "bribery" and "tax evasion."

Instead, the government puts a finishing tarbrush on the final canvas with an inflammatory term of "racketeering" which invites—particularly in the case of a congressman with an Italian-American surname—images of "the Mafia." And while most people simply have no idea of what "racketeering" is in the legal context, they have the presumption that it's quite simply "pretty bad."

In addition, racketeering falls under federal venue and provides additional criminal penalties and provides an additional opportunity to bring the case into a federal court. As such, the case was tightly controlled under federal agents, federal attorneys and a federal judge. As exciting as the "racketeering" charge sounded, it really meant nothing in the entirety of the picture.

In this context, it is important to reiterate—despite the headlines about "Mafia activity" in Youngstown and the Mahoning Valley in Traficant's congressional district—there were never once any allegations in the case against Traficant that there was any kind of "Mafia" or "organized crime" involvement in any of the so-called crimes that Traficant was charged with.

In practically every instance—the exception being the matter of the alleged kickback from Sinclair and the purported tax evasion stemming from the alleged receipt of the kickback—the charges against Traficant involved Traficant doing favors for friends and businesses in his district of the type, as noted, that are standard constituent services and which helped provide employment for many, many people in Traficant's congressional district. Traficant was bringing home the bacon. There was no "Mafia" involvement.

To wrap it up: Even if Traficant was actually 100% guilty of everything that he had been charged with, the fact is that, again, there was nothing whatsoever to do with organized crime in any of those charges and, more importantly, yet again, what Traficant was doing was what every single other member of Congress does. There is no question about that.

The truth is that Jim Traficant was targeted. This was a vindicative targeting in which the government used thoroughly legal transactions of a common sort and made the proverbial "federal case" out of them.

Contrary to what the leading Democrat on the House Ethics Committee—Zionist Congressman Howard Berman (D-Calif.)—said, while publicly joining the lynch mob against Traficant, it was indeed a "conspiracy" involving the FBI and the Justice Department and, as Berman put, "a respected federal judge."

Traficant was targeted.

Traficant was targeted for political reasons.

The charges against Traficant—in comparison to charges brought in recent years against other members of Congress (both before and after Traficant), not to mention cases where charges should have been brought against members of Congress (but were not)—were minimal in nature. They were penny-ante charges.

If Traficant was guilty of anything—which he was clearly not—he was guilty only of such pente-ante charges.

The Justice Department and FBI campaign against Traficant involved those federal law enforcement authorities going back as far as 20 years trying to pry open and uncover virtually every cash transaction in which Traficant had been involved, in one form or another, and trying to find "evidence" that Traficant had accepted cash bribes and favors. However, in all of those years (and millions of dollars in taxpayer money spent, involving perhaps thousands of hours of time expended by government attorneys, accountants and FBI agents) they could only find one cash transaction in which Traficant had been involved, one involving the sale of a horse.

The point is that if Traficant had all of this covert cash that he had received from bribes and other purportedly illegal ventures involving the "racketeering" use of his federal office, the government was unable to show where Traficant was hiding all of these funds or using it in some fashion.

Traficant—never known to be a fashion plate—jokingly pointed out (quite correctly) that he wasn't using all of his alleged cash resources on clothing or jewelry.

He had no mistresses to underwrite. He lived on a run-down houseboat in the Washingon harbor.

The congressman's wife worked as a beautician at home in Ohio, not as a highly paid lobbyist like the wife of one of Traficant's loudest crititcs—Congressman Roy Blunt (R-Missouri)—or as do the wives and family members of other members of Congress.

So the FBI went back 20 years and was unable to find any evidence that Traficant was engaged in cash expenditures that were funded by his purported receipt of under-the-table funds.

All of Traficant's personal transactions during this period (with the apparent notable exception of the purchase of a horse) were done with checks.

CHAPTER EIGHT

Flashback:
A Long-Term Vendetta

It is probably important to note, at this juncture, that, although most people never knew it, during his entire time in Congress, Traficant's congressional salary was being heavily garnisheed by the IRS.

This is interesting and it goes back to the very reason why the Justice Department was determined to "get" Traficant. It goes back to the time when Traficant was Mahoning County sheriff, immediately prior to his election to Congress.

You see, while serving as sheriff, Traficant had been indicted on racketeering charges by the Justice Department which claimed that Traficant had accepted a substantial cash pay-off from a "Mafia" faction in Youngstown in return for a promise not to bring criminal charges against them.

In that original trial, although he was not an attorney, Traficant represented himself against the Justice Department prosecutors and the jury acquitted him on all charges. Like the second case, in which Traficant was convicted, the first case was entirely trumped up.

There was, as noted, a lot of corruption and organized crime activity in Youngstown and its environs, and the fact that Traficant was able to beat the phony charges did not sit well with the FBI and the Justice Department. Then, afterward, Traficant was further vindicated when he won an overwhelming election victory to Congress in the wake of that highly publicized trial.

This further aggravated the anger of his federal enemies—and that is exactly what the Justice Department and the FBI proved to be.

Ironically, although Traficant was acquitted of having taken some $200,000 in bribes from the Mafia faction, the IRS still stepped in and said, "Although Traficant was acquitted of the criminal charge of bribery, he still took $200,000 in cash and he still has the duty to pay taxes on that bribe from the Mafia."Yes, that is (incredibly) exactly what the IRS charged. So although he had been acquitted in criminal court of having accepted the so-called bribe, the federal tax court nonetheless said that Traficant owed taxes on the bribe he had allegedly taken (but which, of course) he had been aquitted in criminal court of having taken!

Here's what happened: during his bribery trial, Traficant admitted that he had, in fact, accepted $200,000 in cash from a Mafia faction. However, he said, he passed that $200,000 on to yet another Mafia faction as part of his own "sting" operation and get evidence against the other organized crime group. Traficant didn't keep the money in question or use it for himself in any way, shape or form. However, the IRS said: "Well, Traficant took the money so therefore he's liable for paying taxes on it. That was income."

As a consequence of this, the IRS put a levy against Traficant and then, when he was elected to Congress, began taking a substantial portion of his congressional salary to fulfill the tax claim! It was all Orwellian, to say the very least.

Now the average American might respond by saying, "Well, Traficant shouldn't have ever taken that money from the Mafia in the first place."

But considering the nature of the beast, particularly a long-standing organized crime presence and influence in the Mahoning Valley, it was inevitable that Traficant—as the chief law enforcement officer in the county—would come up against the mob.

In the bigger picture, however, it must be noted that there are many, many elected officials—local, state and federal—who have regular dealings (and cash arrangements) with organized crime elements and these officials know precisely who they are involved with.

In the Mahoning Valley, it was a way of life—an unavoidable way of doing business—and it would have been surprising if Traficant himself had not ended up being involved with mob elements.

However, the Justice Department decided, at that time, for reasons of its own, that Traficant needed to be brought down—and they failed in their effort (that first time) to do it. And it is again worth noting that Traficant has since said, time and again, that he was fully aware that there were factions within the Justice Department and the FBI operating in that region that were acting illegally in concert with elements of the organized crime networks.

Anyone who believes that some of the most highly regarded members of Congress today have not had dealings with organized crime is kidding himself. The fact is that organized crime is deeply rooted in the American electoral system, reaching all the way to the top.

In any event, Traficant was charged in civil tax court and found liable for back taxes on the alleged "bribe." And that's why his congressional salary was being garnisheed. Traficant was never living high off the hog on his congressional salary, since most of it was being seized by the IRS.

When Traficant was living on his run-down houseboat in the Washington harbor, he did not even have working plumbing! When he needed to go to the bathroom he would go to a nearby restaurant to use its facilities. It's amazing that the Justice Department did not charge that restaurant with "bribing" Traficant.

One of the charges against Traficant, as described in his hometown newspaper, was that he was "bribed" by receiving meals at a "swanky restaurant" in Washington, DC.

The restaurant in question (where this author, Michael Collins Piper, has eaten regularly for some 27 years) is not swanky. People go there in their running clothes. It's a restaurant known for its fine food and excellent service at average Capitol Hill prices.

The implication was that big-time lobbyists were taking Traficant out and spending lots of money on him. Yes, Traficant ate in that restaurant with those lobbyists—lobbyists who were trying to get government contracts that would have employed people in Traficant's district.

Again, what Traficant was doing was no different than what other members of Congress do on a regular basis. But since the government had decided to single out Traficant, target him, "get" him, Traficant's meals with lobbyists were officially transformed, in legal prosecutorial parlance, as "bribes." This was another of the charges against Traficant.

This author has seen Traficant in that restaurant many times over the years, usually dining alone, occasionally with people I knew to be his staff members. And, on a number of occasions, I saw Traficant with others unknown, perhaps those very lobbyists who were allegedly "bribing" him with those dinners at that restaurant.

Although the average person—reading the media accounts of Traficant dining at that "swanky" restaurant— would presume that raucous, fancy meals were in sway, nothing could be further from the truth. In small town America, an average entrée on the menu of a similar restaurant might be $7—but Washington is a lot more expensive.

So Traficant's constitutuents, reading of "swanky" meals, might be astounded by the "high prices" of the meals that their congressman consumed. But those are average Washington prices and certainly didn't reflect any "swanky" meals . . . or bribery.

The bottom line: Jim Traficant is not a crook. The charges against him are trumped-up concoctions of corrupt elements—driven by political motivations—within the ranks of the Justice Department.

There was no forensic, physical evidence against him: no fingerprints, no video recordings, no audio recordings.

Witnesses against Traficant were all people who were

facing possible indictment by the government or who had already been convicted or otherwise pled guilty to other crimes (not related to their dealings with Traficant) and who were seeking favorable treatment at the time of their sentencing in return for testifying against Traficant.

There was even one gentleman who had a "driving under the influence" charge against him whom the federal prosecutors were trying to influence (using the drunk driving charge) in order to get him to testify against Traficant.

So this, on the whole, was the nature of the "criminal" charges that were being levelled against Jim Traficant, charges that had no basis in reality.

However, in the chapter which follows, we will examine a particularly outrageous element in the raft of charges against Traficant that proves, beyond any question, that the case was trumped up, fabricated, founded on lies and deceptions and outright violations of the law.

CHAPTER NINE

The Detore Affair:
The Government Suborns Perjury

One of the most blatant instances of illegal and immoral government pressure against an individual whom they sought to pressure to testify against Traficant involved a gentleman named Richard Detore who had been an official with an aerospace firm known as USAG which was one of the companies that had allegedly "bribed" Traficant.

After Traficant was actually convicted—at the time Congress was pretending to decide whether or not to expel Traficant—Detore testified in televised hearings before the House Ethics Committee that the FBI and federal prosecutor Craig Morford had pressured him, saying, in words to this effect, "You're going to testify against Traficant or you will be indicted for trying to bribe Traficant."

Detore told the FBI and Morford—in words to this effect: "I didn't bribe Traficant nor did I try to bribe him nor do I have any knowledge of any effort by anybody else to bribe Traficant. I haven't committed a crime and I don't know of any crimes committed by Jim Traficant and I'm not going to testify and say that Traficant committed a crime."

What happened to Mr. Detore? He was, in fact, indicted for conspiring to bribe Traficant.

However, Detore did not testify at Traficant's trial because, at that time, he was facing a separate trial in another case and he was urged by his attorneys not to testify.

Although that legal advice may have been justified, in that instance, Detore later charged that his attorneys, in other matters, had otherwise betrayed him and he sought new legal counsel.

Then, afterward, he did testify on Traficant's behalf before Congress when the House Ethics Committee was holding hearings in preparation for the expulsion of

Traficant from the House following his conviction. And, in fact, by doing so, Detore was actually risking his own legal status, since anything he said in that testimony could potentially be used against him in his own upcoming trial.

However, Detore went public, before Congress, and said, essentially, "The only people who are guilty of anything here are the FBI and the Justice Department attorneys who told me that if I didn't lie against Traficant that I would be indicted and possibly be convicted and sent to jail."

Detore had a family, small children, and was under a great deal of emotional pressure and actually considered suicide, facing hundreds of thousands of dollars in legal fees, including funds paid to at least one attorney who sabotaged his defense, apparently in collaboration with the federal authorities. Yet, despite Detore's testimony, the House Ethics Committee voted to recommend that the full House expel Traficant from Congress, which, of course, did indeed happen in the end.

People who saw the testimony said that it was overwhelming to watch and that Detore was clearly telling the truth. And those who have read the testimony concur that the substance of Detore's testimony conclusively pointed toward illegal government maneuvering against Traficant (and Detore) in blatant violation of all standards of the law.

What's interesting about those House Ethics Committee hearings is that the committee chairman, Rep. Joel Hefley (R-Colo.) did everything he could to prevent Traficant from bringing any witnesses to testify on Traficant's behalf. However, the decision had obviously already been made to expel Traficant and no matter how damning the testimony against the Justice Department, the die had been cast.

The committee hearings and the subsequent debate on the floor of the House of Representatives constituted a classic Soviet-style "show trial," a public lynching, a ritual sacrifice. The process was a charade through and through.

The circumstances surrounding Detore's nightmare began when Detore, a test pilot, was fired by J. J. Cafaro, the head of USAG, a Virginia-based technology startup that had contracted to manufacture laser landing technology that Detore had designed and patented. Cafaro was angry that Detore had insisted that Cafaro use government accounting standards at USAG.

At the time of the conflict between Cafaro and Detore, Jim Traficant had been assisting Cafaro's firm by arranging for a demonstration of the technology to the Federal Aviation Administration and for the congressional aviation submittee. Traficant noted that the only agreement he had with Cafaro and USAG was that "the manufacturing of any product would be in my district and eventually the entire corporate headquarters and all [affiliates and subsidiaries] would be relocated to my district for the procurement of jobs for my constituents."

US Attorney Craig Morford, who was the chief prosecutor in the Justice Department's campaign against Traficant, was aware of Traficant's work with Cafaro. And at that juncture, Morford approached Detore with the intent of trying to uncover anything that he (Morford) could use against Traficant regarding the USAG arrangements. However, Detore told Morford that there was nothing inappropriate in Traficant's association with USAG, but, in fact, he did tell Detore of tax fraud and other illegal activities by Cafaro.

However, Morford was not interested in any of that. Instead, he wanted Detore to lie and say that he had overheard Cafaro offering a bribe to Traficant. But Detore refused to lie. In the meantime, Cafaro was facing indictment for having perjured himself in an unrelated criminal case in Ohio involving mob campaign contributions to a former county sherrif. This gave Morford the opportunity he needed to pressure Detore. Morford then arranged for Cafaro to claim that Detore had instigated a scheme to bribe

Traficant. And in return for his testimony against Detore, Morford waived a jail sentence for Cafaro in relation to Cafaro's perjury problems.

Under Morford's direction, Cafaro claimed that he had bribed Traficant with a $13,000 cash payoff after a public event in Youngstown, Ohio, but Traficant had numerous eye-witnesses whose evidence demonstrated that the circumstances as described by Cafaro simply could not have happened in the way he claimed. In short, Cafaro lied.

And Cafaro also claimed that he (Cafaro) had conspired illegally with Traficant to bribe the congressman by arranging for one of his USAG employees to buy Traficant's houseboat in the Washington harbor for an allegedly inflated price as a way of disguising what prosecutor Morford (and Cafaro) said was really a bribe. However, Detore—who was familiar with the negotiations—insisted that there was nothing untoward about those arrangements at all.

To make matters all the more outrageous, Detore learned that his own attorney was secretly collaborating with the federal prosecutor against him (as part of the effort to "get" Traficant) and Detore dismissed his attorney.

However, when Detore went to trial, the jury did not believe Cafaro's testimony against him and Detore was unanimously acquitted.

The bottom line is that the Detore affair, standing alone, demonstrates that the Justice Department, had gone to extraordinary lengths—even including suborning perjury—in order to fabricate a trumped-up criminal case against Jim Traficant. And the irony is that following Traficant's conviction, many of the jurors who voted for his conviction said that they would have not voted to convict him if they had known (during the trial) of what Detore later told Congress.

The Detore affair—standing alone—demonstrates the horrible sham that constituted the entirety of the federal government's "case" against Jim Traficant.

CHAPTER TEN

The Vote for Expulsion:
A Bizarre Ritual Sacrifice

There was only one dissenting vote against Jim Traficant's expulsion from the House of Representatives after his conviction at trial. That vote was cast by then-Rep. Gary Condit (D-Calif.) who had been under siege by the media (and "convicted" in the public eye) because of his personal relationship with a government intern, young Chandra Levy, who had disappeared and was presumed dead.

In fact, what were said to be her bones were later discovered in a Washington park. It was never proven, despite much national frenzy over her disappearance and her relationship with Condit, that the congressman had anything to do with her demise. Condit himself was then defeated for renomination.

All of the major House figures of both parties, along with influential Washington media voices, ranging from *The Washington Times* to *Roll Call*, a weekly journal that focuses on Congress, called for Traficant's expulsion, defaming him as a "crook" and as a "felon."

Roll Call even published a vicious cartoon effectively comparing Traficant with Palestinian leader Yassir Arafat. That was a not-so-subtle jab at Traficant, who had been outspokenly critical of the one-sided U.S. stand in favor of Israel. The same newspaper even smeared a Republican House member from Ohio, Rep. Steve LaTourette, for once having said, "There's isn't a finer man, there isn't a finer member of Congress, there isn't a finer human being ... than Jim Traficant."

In the meantine, in the wake of Traficant's conviction, the major media went out of its way to imply that the jury's conviction of Traficant was somehow unanimous. Evidence points to the contrary.

According to witnesses who were in the courtroom, just before the jury appeared to publicly announce its verdict, several jury members were heard sobbing, as if upset by the decision. Sources say that a number of jurors who were sympathetic to Traficant and who held out for acquittal were badgered and forced into voting for conviction.

The fact that the jury was out so long—despite repeated, confident proclamations by federal prosecutors (and the media) that a "guilty" verdict was never in doubt—demonstrates that the jury did indeed have a tough time reaching its decision.

During the public debate in the House of Representatives over his proposed expulsion, Traficant gave a very emotional defense. His voice was very rough and strained—and no wonder. For hours upon end, Traficant had been lobbying among his House colleagues and then later had to go on the House floor for the public debate, even as many of his colleagues were savaging him.

Traficant, however, had only 30 minutes to be able to speak in order to present a defense against 10 charges involving many picayune details that involved the testimony of many witnesses against him.

The names of the people involved and the specific details of the charges were largely—no, totally—unknown to the American people who bothered to watch the debate on CSPAN. The average American who tuned in to hear Traficant might hear Traficant make reference to the Butchie family. Who were the Butchies? There were references to Sandy Ferrante—an old friend and former employee of Traficant. All of these references, unfortunately, were out of context to the average listener.

The average person tuning in might be inclined to think, "Oh, this is just another crooked congressman trying to get off the hook." Unfortunately, though, the viewers had no idea of the substantial basis for Traficant's defense against the complicated web of charges that had been leveled against him and upon which he had been convicted.

Traficant knew, as did everybody else in Congress, that this was simply a formal process, part of a specific procedure outlined in the House rules, and that this was a ritual sacrifice in the sense it was the culmination of a long-term process that began with the Justice Department's deliberate targeting of Traficant, the trumping-up of charges against him, the collaboration of the media with Justice in promoting the image in peoples' minds that Traficant was involved in criminal activity—even including with "the Mafia."

There had been the transfer of the case outside of Traficant's district, the poisoning of the jury pool in Cleveland by a hostile media in that city, assignment of a judge to the case who had an egregious conflict of interest in the case and who, during the trial, prevented Traficant from introducing exculpatory evidence and witnesses.

In the end, the actual conviction at trial was (to mix metaphors): the colorful bow on the brightly and carefully wrapped package, the icing on the cake: it was all carved in stone. Traficant's expulsion from the House of Representatives was a foregone conclusion.

The members of the House who voted so overwhelmingly for Traficant's expulsion knew they were doing it for one reason and one reason alone: they knew that this is precisely what the powers-that-be wanted done. There are many in the House of Representatives who could be charged with much more serious crimes than Traficant had been, and these members of Congress knew that powerful people have information that could be used against them.

We've all heard about the "secret files" that the late FBI Director J. Edgar Hoover kept on members of Congress (and many others as well) but the truth is that the FBI still keeps such secret files, as do other organizations such as the Anti-Defamation League (ADL) of B'nai B'rith, the Israeli lobby organization that has long collaborated in secret and not-so-secret intrigues with the FBI. These files are used to quietly influence Congress. Everybody in Congress, from the most influential lawmakers to the lowliest staff members, knew that the order of the day was this: "We're getting rid of Traficant. We're done with him. He's gone."

There were several members of Congress who tried to slow down the process, urging that it would be best to come back at a later time to review the matter, but even many of those lawmakers were quick to say they would probably vote to expel Traficant in the end anyway

The July 24, 2002 statement by Rep. Ron Paul (R-Texas) laid forth some of the problems with the heavy-handed push to expel Traficant. Although Paul's statement incorrectly suggested Traficant engaged in misdeeds, the bulk of the statement bears repeating:

Mr. Speaker, many of Congressman Traficant's actions are impossible to defend. Mr. Traficant likely engaged in unethical behavior. I hope all my colleagues would join me in condemning any member who abused his office by requiring staff to pay kick-backs to him and/or do personal work as a condition of employment. I also condemn in the strongest terms possible using one's office to obtain personal favors from constituents, the people we are sent here to represent. Such behavior should never be tolerated.

However, before expelling a member we must consider more than eccentric behavior and ethical standards. We must first consider whether Mr. Traficant's received a fair trial and a fair ethics hearing. His constitutional right to a fair trial, and the right to be judged by those who elected him to office, are every bit as important.

Many Americans believe Congress routinely engages in ethically questionable and unconstitutional actions, actions which are far more injurious to the liberty and prosperity of the American people than the actions of Mr. Traficant.

Some question the ability of Congress to judge the moral behavior of one individual when, to use just one example, we manage to give ourselves a pay raise without taking a direct vote.

Mr. Speaker, after listening carefully to last week's ethics hearing, I have serious concerns about whether Mr. Traficant received a fair trial. In particular, I am concerned whether the change of venue denied Mr. Traficant a meaningful opportunity to present his case to a jury of his peers.

Usually a change of venue is appropriate in cases where the defendant cannot receive a fair trial. I am unaware of any other case where the venue was changed for the benefit of the state.

However, the most disturbing accusations concern the possibility that Mr. Traficant was denied basic due process by not being allowed to present all of his witnesses at the trial. This failure raises serious questions whether Mr. Traficant had the opportunity to present an adequate defense.

These questions are especially serious since one of the jurors from Mr. Traficant's criminal trial told the *Cleveland Plain Dealer* that had he heard the testimony of Richard Detore at Mr. Traficant's trial, he would have voted "not guilty."

Mr. Speaker, I also question the timing of this resolution and the process by which this resolution is being brought to the floor. Mr. Traficant's conviction is currently on appeal. Many Americans reasonably wonder whether the case, and the question of Mr. Traficant's guilt, can be considered settled before the appeals process is completed. I fail to see the harm that would be done to this body if we waited until Mr. Traficant exhausts his right to appeal.

Before voting to expel Mr. Traficant while his appeal is pending, my colleagues should consider the case of former Rep. George Hansen [R-Idaho].

Like Mr. Traficant, Mr. Hansen was convicted in federal court, censured by Congress, and actually served time in federal prison.

However, Mr. Hansen was acquitted on appeal—after his life, career, and reputation were destroyed.

If my colleagues feel it is important to condemn Mr. Traficant before the August recess, perhaps we should consider censure.

Over the past twenty years, this body has censured, rather than expelled, members who have committed various ethical and even criminal violations, ranging from bribery to engaging in sexual activity with underage subordinates.

I also am troubled that Mr. Traficant will have only 30 minutes to plead his case before the full House. Spending only an hour to debate this resolution, as though expelling a member of Congress is no more important than honoring Paul Ecke's contributions to the poinsettia industry, does this Congress a disservice.

In conclusion, because of my concerns over the fairness of Mr. Traficant's trial, I believe it is inappropriate to consider this matter until Mr. Traficant has exhausted his right to appeal.

END OF RON PAUL'S STATEMENT

It was clear that various roles in the dramatic process played out on the floor of the House had been carefully choreographed by the House leadership. It was a tightly-controlled team process.

With few exceptions, it was all too obvious that each member of Congress, particularly the members of the House Ethics Committee, who rose to make a statement, had all been assigned a specific role.

It was clear that they had assembled privately beforehand and each been told what to say about one area of the Traficant case or another in order to provide a unified stand—a united front, so to speak—against Traficant.

The basic argument for Traficant's expulsion—the effort to refute his defenses against expulsion—was laid forth by Rep. Howard Berman, a hard-line advocate for Israel and the ranking Democrat on the House Ethics Committee.

The seedy Mr. Berman puffed up like a big rooster and in his most calculated voice of outrage expressed horror that, "Congressman Traficant is asking us to believe that the FBI and the Justice Department and a respected federal judge engaged in an extended conspiracy against him." In fact, that is precisely what did happen.

And when Traficant did speak before Congress, on the floor of the House, on July 24, 2002, prior to the vote by the House to expel him, Traficant laid it all out in his own inimitable fashion.

CHAPTER ELEVEN

Traficant's Adieu

What follows is a slightly edited transcript of the final remarks that Traficant made on the floor of the House on July 24 prior to the vote to expel him after he was convicted on corruption charges.

Portions of Traficant's remarks have been rearranged for clarity's sake. For example, at different junctures Traficant referred to the shocking case of Richard Detore, who had accused the Justice Department of pressuring him to lie against Traficant under threat of indictment. All of Traficant's references to Detore have been merged together.

Otherwise, this is a faithful presentation of Traficant's often colorful remarks, with additional explanatory material added, as noted.

Ladies and gentlemen, you heard on the ... first national news story that I was involved in a murder [for hire] scheme. It made national headline news. The woman [Sandy Ferrante, who Traficant was supposedly contracting to have killed—Ed.] was a friend of mine. She was so distraught, she called me every name in the book by phone. I didn't know what she was talking about.

She later called and recanted, after they put her in protective custody for eight weeks, paid $800 to keep her dogs in Kentucky, and then brought her to the grand jury twice. And when she said that Jim Traficant committed no crimes, then they demeaned her. But through the process they told her, to ensure her safety, to go public.

Now, if you are a juror and you have heard about Jim Traficant, if that isn't poisoning a voir dire [jury selection process], what is?

The next one in the national news was the $150,000 barn addition. . . . Finally a man with a conscience, Henry Nimitz, sees me at a restaurant and comes up and says, "Jim,

I want to apologize. They were going to indict me, take away my business, ruin my life. My attorney said, why do you have to spend a half a million dollars? Tell them what they want to hear. I did, and I feel like a coward."

But he failed to recognize that I had a friend with me by the name of John Innella. I immediately went back to my office and did an affidavit with John Innella.

Then the next day, as an old sheriff, I called Mr. Nimitz's girlfriend, who admitted that Mr. Nimitz called and admitted what he said to [me].

So now the [claims about the] $150,000 barn was not brought [as one of the charges].

I am going to get right to the point. I want you to imagine there is a small army of patriots, and they are facing a gigantic army armed to the teeth. And the captain, trying to show strength, calls his assistant and says, "Go to the tent and get my bright red vest." He goes and gets the red vest. He puts the red vest on, and he says, "To show the power and courage of our people, without a sidearm I am going to carry this sword and I am going to attack the enemy, and, as they slay me, the blood will not be seen because of my bright red vest and you will be encouraged to fight for our homeland." He gave a banshee cry.

He ran out into battle and was destroyed.

His assistant comes up and he called his attendant. He said, "Go to the tent and get me those dark brown pants."

Think about it.

Tonight I have dark pants on.

Am I scared to death? No. I will go to jail before I will resign and admit to something I didn't do.

Now, I want to go case by case.

Forget all these witnesses.

The judge's husband is a senior partner in the law firm that represented one of the key witnesses [John Cafaro] in my case, and that is part of [my appeal].

My God, if you don't give me a right to appeal a judge whose husband was taking his law firm fees from the Cafaro company . . . then who is our last bastion of appeal if it is not the people's House?

In addition, that person, Cafaro—I am not going to mention names—admitted giving hundreds of thousands of dollars to politicians, I might add, mostly Democrats.

He said he gave me a $13,000 bribe. Because we were at a public meeting, he said he waited until everybody left, and then we walked out together, we got in his car and he gave me the money.

One of the attorneys handling my appeal is a bright young black attorney by the name of Percy Squire, chief clerk to the chief judge of the Northern District of Ohio, and I called him as a character witness.

And he said, "Jim, what do you want me as a character witness for? I came late to that event . . . I walked you out and saw you get in the green truck." Another witness [also] said he picked me up in a green truck . . . And they accepted Cafaro's testimony even though he admitted to lying in a previous RICO trial.

That is one count.

Richard Detore is a patriot. I didn't subpoena Detore because his attorney said, "Don't subpoena Richard, subpoena me." To tell you the truth, I was a gentleman, and I did it. I felt sorry for him.

Before I was indicted, before Detore was indicted, I have a tape where he says everything on that tape that he told the Committee on Standards of Official Conduct [in testimony just days before Traficant's expulsion from Congress].

He said, "Jim, I think I am living in Red China. If I didn't have two kids, I would blow my brains out."

Here is what they wanted Mr. Detore to say: [They wanted him to say] That he was outside the door and heard me and [John] Cafaro make a bribery deal.

What [Rep. Howard] Berman [of California] didn't mention is I paid $10,000 for cars that didn't run, and Mr. Cafaro sold these cars made in Youngstown, the whole company, for $1. They are considered worthless. He owed me money, never gave me the titles [to the cars].

They talked about a Corvette that cost $1,000. It was supposed to be $1,000, but ended up being $6,000 that I paid for it. They said, "Why did you pay so much for the Corvette?" I rented a Corvette because I wanted to get a car to drive to visit [Rep.] John Cooksey [R-La.] to go hunting and to speak at one of his events [in Louisiana].

But he got tied up three weeks later, and I had the car for three weeks, and when I drove back, the license plate expired in 30 days [and I] got picked up on I-395. I ended up paying $6,000 for a car. I paid for it and got the records.

[Cafaro was also] flying members of Congress around—getting senators' girlfriends gifts. But you get out of jail free by "getting" the man right here. [That is, Cafaro cut a deal with the government in a plea bargain agreement in return for testifying that he had "bribed" Traficant.—Ed.]

Mr. Detore, by the way, spent $600,000 and is now without an attorney. His last attorney—[whom] he paid $239,000—went to the judge without him knowing and asked to be withdrawn from the case, because Richard Detore would not give him $100,000.

He had already given him $239,000, and all he did was submit three motions for him.

Someone who impugns the character of Mr. Detore is, in my opinion, violating the sanctity of this House. Because he said . . . "I will not lie. And if they indict me, go ahead and indict me."

The businessman . . . that corroborated Mr. Cafaro's testimony was Al Lang, and I did not find out until after the trial that there was a demand note from Mr. Cafaro to Al Lang to repay the money for the boat he was to buy. . . . Also Mr.

Cafaro paid for Mr. Lang's attorney. So it was really Mr. Lang, and the attorney for Mr. Lang was represented by Mr. Cafaro's attorney.

My God.

After the public [House Ethics Committee] hearings [broadcast on CSPAN], 80 to 90 percent of the viewing public supports my position. All the witnesses that testified against me at trial were either felons or would-be felons, with no physical evidence.

The judge questioned nine of my [defense] witnesses outside the presence of the jury and didn't allow them to testify. The judge didn't allow any of my tapes—and all of my tapes are exculpatory. Even on those who took the Fifth Amendment, she didn't allow them. And one thing rang true:

Every one of the witnesses that testified—[this is] significant—the [prosecutors] had some witnesses scared to death. The key witnesses all would have gone to jail, lost their license, wives would have been indicted, and you know what?

I don't blame any of [them].

In the case of [my] staff, they said one afternoon I invited them down to the boat, they did some sanding—it was a bonding thing—and they drank beer.

The ones that came to the farm, came for the weekend, voluntarily; wanted to use it as a health spa.

[On occasion, members of Traficant's House staff helped Traficant work to restore an aging rickety houseboat that Traficant lived on while in Washington because he could not afford to live elsewhere due to a heavy IRS garnishment of his congressional salary.

[In Ohio, employees of his local district office also helped on Traficant's farm. In both cases, federal prosecutors pressured the employees into saying that Traficant "forced" them to do the work while they were on the federal payroll. Noting could have been further from the truth.—Ed.]

One guy that said he was there 300 times, I had it before the trial, but I heard he took $2,500 to bribe a judge in a DUI case. I thought they had no evidence, and I did not even question him on it.

I have a tape from one of his fellow trustees that I will submit to the committee. [This other trustee] is Jim Price, Weathersville Township, relative to the testimony of that staffer.

Now, let's look at a few affidavits.

Dealing with David Sugar, I just yesterday caught up with him. They said it was a half mile across the state line, and they might now pull me into jail for being out of my district. With one of my staffers close by to listen, Sugar admitted that he told Harry Manganaro that after the second FBI visit, because he had backdated some invoices, if he did not lie against Jim Traficant he would not only be indicted, his daughter, his wife and his son would be indicted.

I have a tape of Harry Manganaro [confirming Sugar's statement that the FBI pressured him to lie against Traficant]. [Manganaro] wasn't allowed to testify, nor was the tape admitted at trial.

In addition to that, a man by the name of Joe Sable told another one of my constituents three days ago, "I feel so bad for Jim. David Sugar told me the same thing" [again, that the FBI pressured him to lie against Traficant].

David Sugar said to me, "Jim, I would love to help you." Now he is saying in the paper, "I never said that to Traficant."

Now, let's talk about Tony Bucci. His fourth plea agreement, his brother in Cuba, fled the country on a fugitive warrant, they sentenced him to six weeks arrest, and here is what he said. He said he did $12,000 worth of work at the Traficant farm, and he "owned" me.

Now, not all of you know me personally, but if you think someone owned me, you would throw me the hell out of here. Witnesses testified that I asked him for jackhammers because we had an old bank barn. I never owned the farm.

But this old bank barn didn't have enough height for horses. I asked him to let me use their jackhammers. He said, "It is an insurance problem. I will send some people out." I said, "I don't want you to do that. You will get too close to that old bank barn and you will drop it in."

And that is what happened, folks. And the whole corner of that barn fell down. Harry Manganaro came out and helped me prop it up. It cost my dad $15,000.

Now, guess what?

Harry Manganaro came to my office yesterday and said his building happened to be firebombed last weekend and all his records are missing, including the bill—$15,000, not counting materials—to my dad who owned [the barn].

When they talk about this [Allen] Sinclair [and the supposed $2,500 per paycheck that Sinclair was supposedly paying to Traficant in a kickback—Ed.] they fail to mention that he had five accounts. And every time he took $2,500 out of one, $2,500 went into another one. And after he left my employment for 22 months, $2,500 didn't go into the other account.

[In other words, the money Sinclair was claiming that he paid in cash kickbacks to Traficant was actually being deposited in another of Sinclair's bank accounts. The trial judge in Traficant's case would not allow Traficant to bring in an expert witness who was able to track Sinclair's financial manipulations in this matter.—Ed.]

And while he was in my employ, he said he earned $50,000 from me and $50,000 from the government. [But even though Sinclair was supposedly paying massive kickbacks to Traficant, Sinclair was still able to buy] a $300,000 house, a brand new Buick van, rented a new car for $300 per month and spent $60,000 on advertising.

[They] said that I took money from companies that did me favors. Look at the testimony of Susan Bucci. She said that [her family] owed me money [and that is why they did work on Traficant's farm in return—Ed.]. I bushhogged 40 acres of their fields every year because her husband, Dan, was sick; and baled 25 acres of his hay every year for five years using my equipment and never charged him. She came to me when [her own] brothers ripped her off.

Now, they said the prosecutor said, "Traficant is touchy-feely. Traficant is too intelligent to be taped." Why didn't they fake body injury [to disguise a hidden microphone]? I have a device that I could tape you right now—your conversation in the midst of all of this [on the floor of Congress]—and you wouldn't know you are being taped.

Now not one wiretap, with the number one target in the United States of the Department of Justice prosecutors?

My phone wasn't tapped?

They didn't want to get an admission?

They didn't want to get Traficant saying, "Listen, go lie to that grand jury."?

If my colleagues know law enforcement and they have got a target, they want a confession, and when they cannot get that confession—I am telling my colleagues this right now: [The FBI and the prosecutors] have more tapes on me than NBC.

Twenty years [of investigating me] and not one tape? Am I that good? Come on.

They didn't bring one FBI or IRS investigator who investigated me to the stand so I could cross-examine them.

They brought a 30-year veteran from Philadelphia. He had seven trips, spent 40 days, a quarter of a million dollars, and all he did was add up the numbers the prosecutor gave him. And said he did no investigation.

When he left, he was so confused he walked into the edge of the jury box, right in the sore spot.

The other one was an FBI rookie.

Now, listen carefully. When it came to fingerprints, the

judge smiled like a fox. She dismissed the jury.

The prosecutor says, "Your honor, we have no finger-prints of the defendant." One thousand documents.

[The FBI investigators] went back 15 years on a horse transaction I had in Uhrichsville, Ohio [with a gentleman named] George Hooker. Everything I paid was by check or a credit card. No cash in 20 years. They could not find one citizen to say Jim Traficant bought a pencil for cash?

Everybody that testified against me would have gone to jail and lost their law license and ruined their life.

A brother-in-law testified that he was taped by someone that he had bribed a county engineer with hundreds of millions of dollars. He told his brother-in-law that he would go to jail for 10 years and lose $15 million, but [the only one the prosecutors really wanted] was Traficant. So he added up all the campaign contributions—which was $2,300 or $2,400—and said he "bribed Traficant."

You know what is amazing about this one? [The judge] didn't even allow the brother-in-law—who was subject to jeopardy, being sentenced in another case—to testify.

And guess what I did?

I used the government's own picture because he said I [accepted the bribe] in a barn. So I held up the picture and said, "What barn was it?" [He] couldn't identify the barn.

I have an affidavit or a tape on every one of these counts.

Sandy Ferrante testified that she personally saw me repay over a period of years money to staffers that I borrowed from them.

When the IRS nailed me, they took me to civil court, and I made $2,400 a month. And that just run out. Now they are going to put me in jail for 12 years, take everything that my wife and I owned, and I never owned that farm.

I will go to jail, but I will be damned if I will be pressured by a government that pressured these witnesses to death to get a conviction on a target—the number one target in the country.

The judge would not let Jim Kirsham, who was an FBI-paid special agent, testify. He was told: "If you get us anything on Traficant, we will build a monument to you."

I got an affidavit from a guy just sent to me from Canada that I helped in a case where 11 Chinese were arrested, and he said, "I want to thank Jim Traficant publicly," and they said, "Stay away from Traficant. Don't mention his name. We are going to get him."

I had an FBI agent that compromised one of my constituents, who was desperately trying to save custody of her child, into sex. She said, "Jim, he didn't throw me to the ground. I don't want my 87-year-old mother to know about it." It was FBI agent [NAME DELETED]. I will be damned if someone is going to rape one of my constituents.

[Note: While Rep. Traficant named the FBI agent in question and we have no doubt that the story is true, we are not publishing the name of the agent. The agent could embroil the publisher in a potentially devastating libel suit.—Ed.]

I got this affidavit today, about an hour before I came here [from] Scott Grodi. He sat through the whole trial [as a juror]. I would like your attention. He was released two days before the trial [when] his aunt died. He said he wanted to finish. I thought we had it resolved for the U.S. marshals to take him so he would be a pallbearer.

When he came back, he was dismissed. He didn't put in his affidavit but you can write and talk to him. He said he knew the prosecutor wanted him out. He said, "I knew Jim Traficant was innocent." He said, "I could see how he impeached their witnesses and how they were lying."

Mr. Grodi said the woman next to him also felt I was innocent. I tried to get an affidavit from her. Her attorney informed us that she was afraid to get involved. Now, folks, if she had something good to say about the government, would he be afraid?

I am not going to get into some of the personal dynam-ics, but there were some people that Mr. Grodi told me that were predisposed to vote against me before that case start-ed, and that upset him. By the way, one of the jurors said, "It's unfortunate [Traficant] got caught, but most of those members of Congress are crooks anyway." I don't think you are crooks.

Now, [Rep. Howard Berman of California told the House during the debate over Traficant's expulsion—Ed.] that there was a recant by Mr. [Leo] Glaser [who had reported earlier to have changed his mind about voting to convict Traficant during the criminal trial.—Ed.]

This is today's newspaper just faxed to me. Mr. Glaser said that he did not recant, and, on the evidence, he could-n't see himself convicting Jim Traficant now.

I have helped everybody in my district and every one of these people, yeah. I did not even like some of them. [My district] had a 22 percent unemployment rate. Did I go to bat for them? Yes. Did I write letters to the secretary of state? Yes. Did I write letters to the secretary of commerce? Yes. Secretary of labor? Yes. Department of transportation? Yes.

But here is where I am at tonight.

I have been pressured for 20 years.

Here is the problem in America. You must take America back. And I am running as an independent, and don't be suprised if I win behind bars.

The American people are afraid of their government.

Why are we afraid of our government?

I am prepared to lose everything. I am prepared to go to jail. You go ahead and expel me, but I am going to tell you [what was said to] Mr. Detore? [The federal prosecutors said to him]: "Do you know what Jim Traficant said about Janet Reno? The administration wants him out."

I said this on radio and [now] I am on the House floor. I

am going to say it to you right now. I called Janet Reno a "traitor" and I believe in my heart she is.

I believe Monica [Lewinsky] and [Former HUD Secretary] Henry Cisneros were not that important, but I think that the Red Army Chinese general giving money to the Democrat National Committee was an affront to our intelligence, and now I am going to tell it like it is:

The Republicans want permanent trade status with China. You [the Republicans] let it slide. Democrats did not want Clinton and the party hurt. You [the Democrats] let it slide. And what you let slide was the freedom of the United States of America. And I called her a traitor.

Nobody should fear our government.

Now, you go ahead and expel me, but you [the Democrats] ran this place for 50 years, and you made the IRS and the FBI and the Justice Department so strong, our people are afraid to death of them.

I want to thank Bill Archer and the Republican Party, and that is why I voted for [Speaker Dennis Hastert in organizing the House following the 2000 election].

For 12 years I tried to change the burden of proof in the civil tax case and protect the American people's homes from being seized, and now, I want to give those statistics because they are relevant to my own case and [this demonstrates why] the IRS hates me for it.

The law was passed in 1998 but the Traficant language wasn't in. Clinton threatened to veto it. Ninety-five percent of the American public wanted the Traficant bill. The Republican chairman, Bill Archer, called me and said he talked to the speaker and leaders and said, "Jim, we are going to put your burden of proof in and we are going to put your language on seizure in the conference," and [Archer] wrote me a letter giving me the credit.

Now, let me give you the statistics that I am proud of and I want to share, because this may be the last time on the floor, and I expect it. The year before compared to the year after the law, wage attachments dropped from 3.1 million to 540,000.

Thank you, Mr. Archer. Thank you, [Rep.] Rob Portman.

Property liens dropped from 688,000 to 161,000, but now let us think of our communities. Seizures of individual family-owned homes dropped from 10,067 to 57 in 50 states when they had to prove it, and you guys did it. Congratulations.

I want to fight these people. I want to fight them like a junkyard dog.

I have a lot of Hispanics mad at me, and I think Ms. [Loretta] Sanchez is a great member, but yes, I voted for [former Rep. Bob] Dornan [to be seated in Congress in a disputed election between Sanchez and Dornan] because I thought we set an illegal precedent by allowing possible illegal immigrants to vote in a federal election.

And I am sorry, but that's the way it is. Now, since then I think you have been an excellent member. If you have been offended by this, I am sorry.

I also want to say this: I urge you to put our troops on our border. I think anybody who jumps the fence shouldn't be made a citizen, they should be thrown out. And you are going to be dealing with homeland security, and I am saddened in my heart I can't vote on it.

The point I am making to my colleagues is I am not unique. I know why I was targeted. I do not need American history to beat them, and I was an embarrassment, and then I brought home John Demjanjuk, [falsely accused of being] the infamous [concentration camp guard] "Ivan the Terrible." I was labeled an anti-Semite. No one would look into his case. The headlines in my paper said that I was a "Nazi sympathizer."

What they did not say [was that] when the [Demjanjuk] family came in, they came to me last because no one would listen to him because they said "the case was too sensitive."

What they also did not print was that I [told the Demjanjuk family]: "If your dad has been convicted, I will go over and pull the switch." Whether he was Ukrainian or Jew made no difference to me.

Through my investigation, I discovered the evidence that proved that [the genuine] "Ivan the Terrible" was nine years older, taller [than Demjanjuk and had] black hair, [and a] long scar on neck and his name was Ivan Marchenko and then presented a picture [of the real Ivan] to the Israeli Supreme Court.

And for all of the people calling me anti-Semite, let me tell my colleagues something: I never voted for a foreign aid bill until we had a surplus, and then I voted for aid. I support Israel, a democratic state, surrounded by a cluster of monarchs and dictators who have held us hostage for oil.

But he was not Ivan, and the Israeli Supreme Court taught me something that I think Congress should know. They delivered him to me on an El Al flight to take home.

Congress would not even hold a hearing in light of my compelling evidence that the Israeli Supreme Court freed him, because it was "too sensitive."

What has happened to us, Congress?

Am I different? Yeah. Have I changed my pants? No.

Deep down my colleagues know they want to wear wider bottoms; they are just not secure enough to do it. I do wear skinny ties. Yeah, wide ties make me look heavier than I am and I am heavy enough.

Do I do my hair with a weed whacker? I admit.

Take into consideration what my colleagues are doing.

Former Congressman Michael Myers: an FBI undercover agent posing as an Arab sheik gave him $250,000, captured by videotape, and my colleagues [suspended expelling him from the House] till after the break. The two members who violated a 17-year-old page boy [then-Rep. Gerry Studds] and a 17-year-old page girl [then- Rep. Dan Crane]—which is rape in every state—were not expelled.

I did nothing wrong. Go ahead and expel me. I believe this judge is so afraid of what is resonating throughout America—citizens who believe that they should not have to fear their government and that Congress is the last hope to take it back. I am saying to the speaker, take it back.

No American should fear their government and this guy does not. I am ready to go. Expel me. It will make it easier for them to really "jack" me good.

But do my colleagues know what they will have done?

They will have taken the standards of a RICO case down to less than a DUI where a person needs a .10 level to get a conviction.

Let me tell my colleagues what happened to me early Saturday morning . . . [Traficant then described being stopped by local police officers in Ohio and forced to go through a variety of tests to see if he was driving drunk.— Ed.] [After going through the tests] here is what I asked them: "Did the FBI tell you that was my car and ask you to see if you can get a DUI on me?"

They looked at each other, and [because of House decorum] I cannot [say] exactly what I told them but I told them if I find out it is an FBI agent that did it, I will tear his throat out, and if they lied to me, I would come back to them and tear their throats out.

They are not going to frighten me. I am ready to go to jail. I will go the jail before I admit to a crime I did not commit. And there was never any intent to commit a crime.

I am convinced this judge is going to put me in jail. She cannot stand my guts. And she is deathly afraid of me getting on national TV, because it is beginning to resonate around the country about how people fear our government. And why do we?

You know, there is something unusual here. You did not

elect me. Yes, you have the right to throw me out. My people do not want me out. There is something that was not allowed to be brought, and I give the gentleman from Colorado (Mr. Hefley) and the committee great respect. But ladies and gentlemen, you passed a 1967 Jury Service and Selection Plan in the Northern District of Ohio before Traficant was indicted, passed a jury selection plan that was not ratified until after my indictment. They excluded people from my area that knew me and these witnesses from the jury pool.

It is not a matter of liking me. A lot of members do not like me . . . But I want your vote . . . I want to be able to go up and I want to fight the Department of Justice and the IRS . . . I want you to think of this: There may come a time when you might get targeted.

You know what I was told? "Watch what you say. You are too outspoken. Shut up about the Reno case."

I am not going to shut up. I want your vote because I think my vote is your vote, and my people elected me and I do not think you should take their representative away.

With that, thank you. . . .

So it was that Jim Traficant bade farewell to his colleagues who so enthusiastically (or so it seemed) joined in the lynch mob in committing the Ritual Sacrifice of Jim Traficant.

And bear in mind the irony that more than a few of those lawmakers later became the subject of federal corruption inquiries—some of which are still ongoing. One of them—Republican Randy "Duke" Cunningham of California—is now in jail. Others may well end up there themselves.

Perhaps now some of those who face prosecution and possible jail time might realize what Jim Traficant was talking about. Are they "guilty" as they concluded Traficant had been? Maybe. But maybe not.

CHAPTER TWELVE

Standing Up to the Judge:
Speaking Truth to Power

In sentencing Jim Traficant to jail, federal Judge Lesley Wells seemed primarily concerned about the fact that Traficant had dared criticize the government in fending off the criminal indictment against him.

"You sneered at the entire calling of public service with your remarks," said Wells. "Using the national and local media, you mocked [government institutions]. You attacked all federal judges as tools of the Justice Department."

Calling Traficant a demagogue, the judge even compared him with Adolf Hitler when she dredged up the technique of "the big lie," long incorrectly attributed to having been advocated by Hitler. Wells told Traficant: "The truth is rarely in you. Your drumbeat is the drumbeat of a big lie, an old tactic . . . If you tell a lie often enough, people will believe it."

Wells even managed to denounce yet another favorite media bugaboo—so-called "conspiracy theories"—in sentencing Traficant.

Echoing Rep. Howard Berman (D-Calif.) who said that it was ridiculous to think that either government officials or "a respected federal judge" (namely, Judge Wells) would engage in any kind of conspiracy to "get" Traficant, Wells claimed that people believe Traficant "because it suits their predisposition to believe conspiracy theories."

At the sentencing, joining Wells in declaiming against those who believe in such ugly theories and denouncing any form of criticism of the government, the Assistant U.S. Attorney who prosecuted Traficant, Craig Morford, complained that Traficant was "demean[ing] this nation's institutions" and that Traficant's claims of government misconduct were so "dangerous" because—as Morford sobbed, "they fan the passions of some people who believe these claims."

Morford even used the tired-and-worn "rally round the

flag" gimmick and summoned up the ongoing war on terrorism, declaring that "This is a critical time in our nation's history. Terrorism threatens an explosion from abroad, moral implosions from within."

Even while standing before the judge that held his fate in her hands, Jim Traficant wouldn't bend. Most people would be cowed by a federal judge about to pass sentence on them. Not Traficant.

While Judge Wells was sentencing Traficant to jail, the no-nonsense congressman lashed out at her. "You did not give me a fair trial," he said, interrupting the judge. "You even had an unfair jury before me, and you know it." Traficant wouldn't shut up:

> I charge the prosecution with subornation of perjury. I'm being called the crook here. You pressured Americans, and the loss of public trust in government is not because of Jim Traficant, it is because of you. You're just like those attorneys who were willing to let John Demjanjuk die in Israel, and I can't stand looking at you.
>
> This trial is a microcosm of what's happening in America. People distrust the courts. I'll be damned if the government has become so strong that they'll scare the American people to death. I'm not ashamed of a damned thing.

At least one spectator during the sentencing seemed to be quite satisfied with Traficant's jail sentence.

This was one of those jurors who had voted to convict Traficant: Mrs. Jeri Zimmerman of Cleveland, who—according to the anti-Traficant *Cleveland Business Journal*—nodded her head in agreement with the judge as she maliciously attacked Traficant.

According to one source who had inside knowledge of

the Traficant affair, Mrs. Zimmerman was "the big catalyst" inside the jury against Traficant and who—by sheer force of personality—was certainly the one person who swayed the jury against Traficant. And she had a bias against Traficant.

Mrs. Zimmerman is Jewish. This is significant for it is a known fact that many members of the Jewish community in the Cleveland area (where the trial was held) were fiercely hostile to Traficant.

What's interesting about Traficant's performance in court the day he was sentenced is this: when other members of Congress have been convicted of crimes and faced sentencing, they have uniformly told the court: "I'm so sorry. I've let my friends and family down. I've let my dog down. I've let my constituents down. I've let my congressional colleagues down. I've let my country down. I've let everybody in the whole world down. Most of all, I've let myself down. I realize now that I have to pay my debt to society for violating the rules of the House and the laws of our nation. Please forgive me if you can. And, oh yes, don't give me too long a sentence, and, if you can, please don't sentence me to jail at all. Give me probation. Give me community service. I won't do it again."

However, Jim Traficant didn't do that. No, Traficant responded and reacted like an innocent person who has been charged with and convicted of crimes he did not commit. Traficant stood up and shouted at the judge and shouted at the prosecution and said, "I'm not guilty. I shouldn't be here. You fixed this trial against me. You arranged the evidence against me. You wouldn't let me present an effective defense. I'm not guilty and the reason why my friends across America are mad as hell is because you are framing me, just like you've framed other people all over his country."

Traficant stood up. He didn't cower in front of a hostile judge who he knew was clearly ready to send him away for an extended prison sentence. Traficant could have shut up, but, instead, he was challenging, in no uncertain terms, the very person who, conceivably, could have given Traficant a brief prison term accompanied by several years of probation. Traficant continued to fight, like the fighter he has always been. He was an innocent man, as he said. The evidence indicates that he was—and is—innocent and he was not about to give up, even at that last moment before his sentencing.

And in the days following the trial and the sentencing, former jurors were acknowledging that there was "reasonable doubt" in at least some of the charges against Traficant and that if they had heard some of the evidence that Traficant had sought to introduce (but which the judge prevented him from doing), they would not have convicted him on those counts. The jurors only found out about that evidence after the trial.

The judge would not even let Traficant out on bail prior to the hearing of his appeal. Traficant was a non-violent person with no prior convictions—a member of Congress no less, and a former law enforcement officer.

Federal Judge Wells sentenced him to report to jail immediately, implying that Traficant was a possible "flight risk," a highly unlikely suggestion considering the fact that Traficant was on the ballot as an independent candidate, still seeking re-election to Congress. Yet, on July 30, 2002, the judge sent him straight to jail.

CHAPTER THIRTEEN

Traficant Speaks From Jail:
Unbowed and Unbending

This author, Michael Collins Piper, had the proud distinction of being the only journalist on the face of the planet to whom Traficant agreed to speak while he was being held in a county jail in Ohio prior to being transferred to federal prison.

As this is written, nearly six years later, I remain the only journalist to whom Traficant has spoken from jail, despite the fact that there were literally hundreds of interview requests coming in from such prestigious media outlets as *The New York Times*, *The Washington Post* and other big names in the elite media.

Traficant knew that *The Spotlight* and later *American Free Press* (the journals for which I covered the Traficant case) were the only publications anywhere that had provided fair coverage—and presented his side of the story. While The Washington Post was snidely speculating as to whether Traficant would be permitted to wear his toupee in prison, we were providing solid details about his defense against these trumped-up corruption charges.

When *The Washington Post* finally did publish any details about the specifics of Traficant's defense against the charges, it was not in the news section, but instead in the gossip section, buried in the midst of a "personality" piece, saying, essentially, "Oh, here's Traficant's last hurrah."

When I contacted the jail and asked to interview Traficant, he called me back and said, "*American Free Press* is the only newspaper I'm talking to."

Traficant had a special message to AFP readers: "The readers of *American Free Press* need to know about those polls that show that I can get elected and that I have a lot of support out here. I think I can be—and I want to be—the first American ever elected to Congress from a prison cell."

The imprisoned ex-congressman believes (and he's right) that his re-election to Congress—even while sitting in a federal prison—would send a message loud and strong that citizens are fed up with government misdeeds and all-around disdain for the hard-working productive people of middle America.

"People fear the government, and no one should fear the government," said Traficant. "And when you start fearing your government, you end up hating your government. America is building in a hell of a problem, and it has got to be changed."

Although the media was repeatedly suggesting that if Traficant was sent to a federal prison outside the boundaries of his home state that he would not be eligible to seek office from Ohio, this was not necessarily the case at all.

Traficant told AFP that "I think they are working to try to keep me off the ballot, but I don't think they can. The Constitution says that you must be an inhabitant of the state. The town that I returned to, when I left Washington, is in Ohio. That's where I'm an inhabitant.

"That legal argument needs to be heard by people who want to support my campaign. If the federal authorities do move me out of state, I think I can still get around that."

Traficant's attorneys fully intended to raise all legal questions pertinent to the matter if Traficant was placed in a prison outside of his home state (which he ultimately was).

In the meantime, however, even Traficant's Republican opponent, Anne Benjamin admitted to *The Cleveland Plain Dealer* that she understood from Ohio state election officials that Traficant was still eligible to run for Congress from an out-of-state prison cell.

In addition, the *Plain Dealer* pointed out, any attempt to remove Traficant from the ballot would have to come from Trumball County (Ohio) officials and thus far, according to the director of the county's board of elections, there was no intention of questioning Traficant's ballot status.

In any event, because there is a federal facility not far from Traficant's home town of Poland, the decision to place Traficant in Pennsylvania probably caused many people who had been otherwise skeptical to start thinking that Traficant's allegations of a conspiracy against him may have some validity after all.

About the role the FBI and the Justice Department played in his prosecution, Traficant commented succintly: "They pressured people to lie like you can't believe. There's no physical evidence. Not one bit of corroboration. Not one fingerprint. Nothing."

In his interview with AFP, Traficant summarized the fashion in which the judge, Lesley Wells, handled his case from her position on the bench.

> I wasn't allowed to bring any evidence. The judge didn't allow me to bring nine witnesses before the jury. But she made them testify before her, with the jury out of the room.
>
> The judge didn't allow me to introduce ten tapes that provided evidence of my innocence. She kept those tapes away from the jury. She tied my hands behind my back. But to tell you the truth, I damned near beat her and the prosecutors without that evidence.

Traficant refused to back off on his repeated charge that federal authorities—including former Attorney General Janet Reno—were out to "get" him:

> They had to get rid of me. [One witness] Richard Detore described how the federal prosecutors brought up Janet Reno to him [and pointed out how Traficant had criticized

her]. I'm the only one that went after Janet
Reno. The Republicans wanted free trade with
China and the Democrats didn't want Clinton
to get hurt.

So I was the only one going after Reno and
she went after me like a ton of bricks.

Traficant elaborated on some of the controversial stands
that he took while serving in Congress, inflaming the political establishment:

Why are they so afraid to death of me? I'm
the only one that's talking about trade, talking
about giving away the country, about China
and about China slipping in money to the U.S.
government and the godamned politicians are
getting away with it. Our borders are wide
open and then they talk about terrorists and
narcotics coming across.

"My issues," Traficant noted, "are not popular with the
government but they are popular with the people."

Traficant's campaign platform was based on a theme
that is certain to rattle the cages of those who thrive on big
government and federal power:

No one should fear their government.

My campaign platform is that there's no
freedom in America. You are born into a partnership with Uncle Sam.

They're the company store and they own
your soul.

Why should we fear our government? I'm
gonna throw those sons of bitches out.

Traficant was particularly proud of his work in reforming the tax laws, especially those governing the Internal Revenue Service and its relationship with the American taxpayers. "I'm the one that changed all the IRS laws," Traficant pointed out. "But," he noted, "the press has never reported this." The ex-congressman cited some of his specific accomplishments to AFP:

> I'm the one that passed the law that says a citizen can sue the IRS for $1,000,000 if they abuse you. That's one of my laws. Secondly, I changed the law regarding burden of proof in a civil tax case. You used to be considered guilty and had to prove yourself innocent. The third thing is that under one of my IRS reforms, the IRS can no longer seize your property without a court order.
>
> Here are some statistics. After my laws passed, wage attachments dropped from 3.1 million to 540,000. Property liens dropped from 688,000 to 60,000. Seizures of individual family-owned homes dropped from 10,067 to 57 in the entire country. Can you believe it?

However, Traficant had a lot more in mind: "When I get back into Congress—and I can do it with the help of people around the country—I'm going to introduce a bill to eliminate the IRS and create a 15% national retail sales tax, exempt everybody at the poverty level. Everybody else would pay the sales tax.

"The fact is," said Traficant, "There's no freedom in America. That's a joke. You are born into a limited partnership with the Internal Revenue Service. I want that to be quoted," he emphasized.

Traficant added: "That's my goal now: to abolish the Sixteenth Amendment and to abolish the IRS and to replace it by creating a 15% national retail sales tax."

In reference to his sales tax proposal (which had great appeal to many voters) Traficant pointed out:

> Harvard has done a study saying that, with a sales tax, prices won't even increase because the tax code is what's putting all the costs on American products in the first place.
>
> When you do that, and create this program with the national retail sales tax, even the drug dealers on the street start paying this tax.
>
> But they aren't paying the income tax.
>
> Ninety percent of all retail sales taxes are collected by nine percent of retailers.
>
> My proposal would even exempt yard sales up to $10,000 for individuals.
>
> You are not getting hit twice like you do when you buy a car: when you sell it, you pay another sales tax.
>
> This way, when you buy a car, you pay a 15% sales tax. But when you sell it, the buyer pays the 15%. There's no double taxation under my proposal."
>
> Today, twenty-four percent of the cost of an American automobile is in taxes. Then when it is sent overseas, it is hit with a value-added tax.
>
> No wonder we have a trade deficit.

And speaking of the trade issue—another key concern of the populist congressman who was a modern-day trailblaizer on the issue—Traficant added:

I want to put a five percent tariff on the imported goods from any country that has a lower standard of living than the United States or any country which keeps our products out. China, for example, has a 17 cents an hour labor wage. Japan doesn't let our products in. I want that five percent and then we can [eliminate Social Security withholdings from the paychecks of wage-earners].

This way American companies will move back to America. You can't blame American companies for leaving with the oppressive tax code that we've got.

Traficant also intended to continue working for reform of the federal law enforcement system that has put him in federal prison and which has been responsible for travesties such as Waco and Ruby Ridge:

As for the FBI and the Justice Department, I'm going to put in legislation to have an independent agency, appointed by the president for ten years and approved by the Senate. Their job will be nothing but to investigate the serious cases like Waco, Ruby Ridge— cases like that. Right now the Justice Department has its own Office of Professional Responsibility, but that's nothing more than "damage control" for the Justice Department.

Traficant had an explanation for the unusually close relationship between federal judges and the FBI and the Justice Department that is quite accurate:

"Remember," he pointed out, "these judges are afraid of the FBI and the IRS. The reason is this: Although Congress can impeach federal judges, it is not Congress that investigates these federal judges before they are appointed. It is the FBI and the IRS that do it. And it's the FBI and the IRS that bring all of these cases to the federal judges, and they do what the FBI and the IRS want them to do. So they're all against me."

As far as Judge Wells is concerned, Traficant reminds people: "The judge's husband is an attorney for Squires, Sanders & Dempsey in Cleveland. That firm handled business for the firm of John Cafaro who was a key government witness against me. Judge Wells shouldn't have even been the judge in my case. That's a Hell of a story in itself."

Although the judge refused to allow Traficant to remain free on bail and refused to grant him a new trial, Traficant appealed his conviction before the Sixth U.S. Circuit Court of Appeals—but as we know now, the court refused to overturn his conviction.

And even though he was running as an independent— sitting in a jail cell—Jim Traficant proved still popular with the voters in his home district. He won fully 15% of the vote, quite a remarkable percentage (all things considered) and a real tribute from his many friends and admirers.

CHAPTER FOURTEEN

Rewarding the Real Criminals—
And Trying to Destroy the Traficant Family

Although it was Janet Reno's Democrat-dominated Justice Department that first initiated the criminal investigation that ultimately sent Jim Traficant to jail, Republican Attorney General John Ashcroft eagerly kept Reno's inquiry in place when he assumed office and brought it to its fateful conclusion.

Adding insult to injury Ashcroft publicly honored the team that handled Traficant's prosecution—despite widespread perception (documented in these pages)—that Traficant was "set up" by the FBI and the Justice Department in the first place.

The Traficant tormenters being awarded with the Attorney General's Award for Distinguished Service were two FBI special agents, Richard Mark Denholm II of the FBI's Criminal Investigative Division and Michael Pikunas of the bureau's Cleveland office.

Craig Morford, the assistant U.S. Attorney who had been the lead prosecutor in the Traficant trial, and Bernard Smith and Matthew Kall, assistant U.S. attorneys for the Northern District of Ohio, also received the award.

Although Traficant was now sitting in federal prison at Allenwood in Pennsylvania (later transferred to the federal prison in Rochester, Minnesota) his attorneys were appealing his conviction even as those who orchestrated his unjust conviction were being heralded for their crimes.

This came at the same time that the Justice Department continued its campaign to harass Traficant's wife and daughter, attempting to seize their assets as part of a claimed effort to collect federal fines that were levied on Traficant—not his wife and daughter—when he was sentenced to prison.

Further proceeding in their long-standing efforts to

smear Traficant,hostile newspapers in Ohio falsely suggested to readers that Traficant had "misbehaved" while incarcerated, saying Traficant "refused to work in the kitchen."

The implication, of course, was that the ex-congressman considered such work beneath him. However, the truth is that Traficant refused an offer to work in the prison kitchen because he knew there were other prisoners ahead of him in line to get such a "cushy" job and he wouldn't take advantage of his fame and position. For his refusal, Traficant was thrown in "the hole."

Traficant himself told *American Free Press*, in a letter written shortly after he was jailed, that he had, in fact, been consigned to the prison "hole" for refusing to accept special "plum" prison work assignments ahead of other prisoners who were on waiting lists for those jobs before Traficant. In short, the ex-congressman refused special treatment and, for doing so, was punished by the prison authorities.

Critics suspect this was a deliberate effort by prison authorities to create strife between Traficant and other prisoners who may have potentially resented Traficant, a former congressman.

However, Traficant refused to take the bait and then was punished for having done so.

Meanwhile, the federal authorities began moving quickly to collect a $150,000 fine levied against Traficant following his conviction.

The government also moved to collect nearly $100,000 in additional funds that the FBI and the Justice Department falsely claimed Traficant accepted in bribes and failed to pay taxes on.

Since Traficant was no longer receiving a salary, the FBI and the Justice Department were trying to squeeze the money out of Traficant's wife Tish, who works as a beautician, and from his daughter, Elizabeth Chahine, who worked as a clerk for the state of Ohio. The government was suggesting that Traficant's wife and daughter were holding assets that actually belonged to Traficant.

Under court order, the two women were subpoenaed to appear before federal authorities with the following wide-ranging list of materials:

• Copies of federal income tax returns for the previous three years.

• All documents showing ownership of personal or real property belonging to Jim Traficant with a value of more than $100.

• All titles, deeds, mortgages and other documents evidencing their ownership in real estate and the dates they acquired such ownership.

• All leases, notes receivable, mortgage, liens, contracts, judgments and other documents evidencing income, dividends or royalties owed or paid to them.

• All records, including pay stubs evidencing gross wages, salary or commissions for the past six months.

• All records establishing ownership in all or part of any business as sole owner, partner or stockholder and the financial condition of such business for the past three years including a statement of assets, inventories, liabilities, gross and net income and the amount of any undistributed profits in the business.

• All titles and registrations for all motor vehicles owned in whole or part by Jim Traficant. All titles and registrations for all motor vehicles transferred to them by him.

• All receipts, appraisals and other statements or documents establishing ownership and value of jewelry and furs owned by them and/or their business.

• Statements for all their checking, savings and trust accounts for the previous 12 months.

• All records and statements for certificates of deposit ,savings bonds, stocks, bonds, coupons and mutual funds they and/or their business may own, separately or jointly with the imprisoned ex-congressman.

• All life insurance policies in effect and all records evidencing their face value and cash surrender value where the named insured is Jim Traficant and they are the beneficiary.

• All records establishing them and/or their business interest in any account held by someone else on them and/or their business behalf in any bank, savings institution or credit union.

• All records evidencing their ownership and/or their business interest in any property, real or personal, in the possession of or name of any person or corporation.

• A list of all their and/or their business's real property transferred by gift, sale or otherwise since Feb. 1, 2002 and all records establishing the transfer and the value received.

• All records evidencing their receipt of any pension, disability compensation, retirement pay or other benefits from the United States or any other source on behalf of Jim Traficant.

Clearly, the federal authorities were not content with having imprisoned Traficant. Now they were harassing his family—with a vengeance.

And although the federal Bureau of Prisons originally announced that Traficant's expected release date—assuming his conviction was not overturned—was July 17, 2009. for reasons which the bureau will not explain, Traficant's new release date was extended to August 10, 2009.

In the meantime, the Justice Department is seizing $770.50 each month from Traficant's congressional pension, not to mention an additional $50 monthly in funds from Traficant's prison work earnings. The money being seized is being applied by the federal authorities to the $150,000 fine levied against Traficant upon his conviction.

The last straw came in 2007 when the Assistant U.S. Attorney who staged the trumped-up prosecution of Traficant, Craig Morford, was temporarily promoted to the post of acting Deputy Attorney General—the number two position at the Justice Department in Washington. And although Morford was forced to give up the post when a permanent replacement was found to fill the slot, the promotion—by President George W. Bush—was clearly a boon to Morford's career.

However, steadfast supporters of Jim Traficant—who know full well that the congressman was unlawfully convicted—have worked to expose Morford in postings on the Internet. They have established a fact-filled (and thought-provoking) website at craig-morford.com, which outlines Morford's misconduct in the Traficant affair.

In addition, there are several other websites that feature Morford's antics, along with other information relating to the Traficant case (as well as Traficant's remarkable career). These sites include:

- traficant-update.com
- traficant.com
- freetraficant.com
- beammeupart.com

This last website is particularly interesting in that it makes available for sale to the public a variety of paintings that the former Congressman has done while in prison. Proceeds from the sale assist Traficant's family.

So it is that while Jim Traficant sits in federal prison and his family struggles to survive, the federal criminals who orchestrated his conviction move on with their careers, even as the Justice Department pursues its vendetta against Traficant and his family.

This is "justice" in America.

CHAPTER FIFTEEN

Letter From a Political Prisoner

What follows is the text of a letter that Jim Traficant wrote from prison to one of his supporters, illustrating that—as noted before—Traficant remains unbent and unbowed. The letter speaks for itself. Those who read the letter should note that Traficant concludes by providing his wife's address for those who wish to write her to provide their support.

Dear (Name Withheld),

Thank you! Thank you for thinking of me and my family. Life is hectic and fast-paced-- and for you to have thought of me, and then to stop and take time from your precious life to write me-- is an honor. And once again, I thank you!

Most of the people who write me say they cannot understand why the government targeted me with such a passion. Every rumor and innuendo that any political opponent would plant and foster became public and, before long, developed into an indictment without any physical evidence-- only the testimony of subjects who were able to avoid jail by fabricating falsehoods about me. Lies and half-truths became "facts" and ultimately became a 10 count indictment.

My evidence, that would have proved they were lying, was not allowed to be presented, either before the Congress or the Federal Court! However, I know why I was targeted: I was not afraid of the government, and I had learned too much!

The beginning of all of this was my first trial, in 1983, when I became the only American in history to defeat the U.S. Department of Justice in a RICO case *pro se* (representing myself), and me not being an attorney. They were embarrassed! The straw that broke the camel's back was when I proved that John Demjanjuk was not the infamous

"Ivan the Terrible" of the Treblinka death camp in Poland. The government was stunned and in shock. The real Ivan was nine years older, taller, and had black hair and a scar on his neck; his name was Ivan Marchenko.

My investigation, in conjunction with John Demanjuk's beautiful family, proved not only that John was innocent, but also that the Justice Department knew he was not guilty–even before they took him to court!

Shame, shame!! They lied to the court—gave false testimony and presented false witnesses—knowing that he would be put to death! Shame!! The Justice Department then came after me with revenge, and a passion! I lost my respect and my faith in our government. Because this case was "too sensitive," Congress would not even hold a hearing on my evidence . . . Congress, all of them, at the time, turned their back, worried about reelection!!

The Democrats were in charge then, and they knew of my investigation in Congress . . . hoping I would abandon it! I did not! I sent my findings to the Israeli Supreme Court and they had no choice: They released John Demjanjuk! In fact, they delivered him to me at the airport in Tel Aviv, Israel, and I personally brought him home, along with his son, his son-in-law, and Israeli bodyguards!

I am proud of what I did. No one else, in the House or the Senate, would even talk to the family, afraid of media power and the vindictiveness of the Justice Department. But even today, John Demjanjuk is still being persecuted.

Shame!

The government agents that destroyed Demjanjuk's life should be in jail! That was just the tip of the iceberg. When people saw what I had done for the Demjanjuk family they came to me with unbelievable information.

The information is so powerful that it is hard to believe, and the government knew I was getting sensitive information that could damage the American people's confidence in the government.

People came to me with facts about Waco, Ruby Ridge, Pan Am Flight 103, Jimmy Hoffa, and the assassination of President John F. Kennedy. It may all sound far-fetched, but I do know what happened to Hoffa and JFK.

The government knows that I know-- and so they had to ruin my voice by destroying my credibility. I may yet divulge this information if I can get the proper forum.

As you know, I was the dreaded enemy of the IRS. My legislation in the last IRS Reform Bill changed the Burden of Proof law. Before that, you had to prove you were innocent in a tax court. The burden of proof was on the taxpayer. The IRS said you owed . . . but the IRS. did not have to prove it. Unbelievable!

Now that the IRS has to prove their charges, the following statistics tell the true story. Comparing One Year Before the changes to One Year After:

1. Wage Garnishments dropped from 3.1 million to 560,000;

2. Taxpayer Property Liens dropped from 680,000 to 161,000;

3. Foreclosures on individual family-owned homes dropped from 10,063 to 57! That's right: only 57 homes in all 50 states!

Fact is, the IRS was seizing our homes—over 10,000 every year—when they had neither proof nor the right to do so! Congress allowed the IRS. to intimidate us and frighten us.

Think about it! And then maybe you can begin to understand why I love America but hate the Government and why the Government hates me. The Justice Department had to get rid of me, but I'll be damned if I would back down!

America is in trouble . . . not from without, but from within! The Central Government has become too powerful. Citizens fear the Government. This is wrong. This is dangerous! I know the Government covered-up and promulgated LIES about Waco, Ruby Ridge, Pan Am Flight 103, Hoffa, and JFK. The Government knew I was right when I called Janet Reno a traitor. Janet Reno sold us out when she refused to investigate a $10-million payoff to the Democratic Party from a general in the Red Chinese Army (no less!).

Think about it! And the Government knew that I had known why Reno was forced to betray America!

I'm proud that I tried to do something about it! Someday the truth will come out. (I hope China never attacks us!)

Many of you have asked what you can do for me. I appreciate this. You can help my family:

Mrs. Tish Traficant
429 N. Main Street
Poland, OH 44514

Thank you for remembering me, for thinking of me . . . for caring!

God Bless!

Jim Traficant

AFTERWORD:

The Tip of the Iceberg . . .

Congressman Jim Traficant was most assuredly lynched by the Justice Department just as if he had been taken by force and hanged from a lamp post near the U.S. Capitol in Washington—a method of justice that certainly should be applied to many of the corrupt individuals who continue to misrule America from their positions in Congress and throughout official Washington.

However, what happened to Traficant—as we said at the outset—could happen to any American should he or she fall into the gunsights of the powerful forces that reign supreme in America.

The Traficant case is the proverbial tip of the iceberg, for the truth is that sitting alongside Traficant in prisons today—federal, state and local—there are probably thousands of Americans who were as much victims of an unjust system as Traficant.

These people, too, are political prisoners in the plainest and most very real sense of the word. But we haven't heard about these folks because they didn't have the high public profile of the outspoken Jim Traficant.

So the lesson to be learned is very simple:

Even someone in a position of influence—such as a U.S. Congressman—can be railroaded into prison by the very people whose job it is to enforce the laws.

The assembly of this book—like its reading—has been most uncomfortable for the fact is that all of the information within these pages is an ugly reflection of the state of affairs in which the people of this country must now recognize that their nation has arrived.

The shocking public suicide in 1987 of Pennsylvania State Treasurer R. Budd Dwyer who had been hailed by everyone—except by corrupt forces inside the Justice Department—as a decent and honest man should have exposed, once and for all, the dangerous sinkhole which our so-called "Justice" Department had become, but few people heeded Dwyer's final words when he called out for the public to become aware of the manner in which the legal process can be used by venal personalities to carry out political vengeance.

The beleaguered Dwyer died a hero, not as a coward as some might have suggested. Dwyer literally gave his own life in the hope that his suicide—before a crowded press conference—would force the media to tell his story.

Perhaps naively—not really recognizing how corrupt the media itself really is—Dwyer hoped and believed that his suicide would compel the media to reveal to the public how his prosecution had been fabricated and manipulated, but the media refused to do it, very much in the same fashion as—years later—the media not only refused to permit Jim Traficant's side of the story to be heard but also actively aided and abetted the corrupt elements in the Justice Department that were determined to destroy Traficant, just as others in that same federal law enforcement agency had done to Budd Dwyer.

So it is that the final pages of this volume will be dedicated to an overview of the tragic Dwyer case, first published in 1987 in *The Spotlight* newspaper, the only newspaper that took up Dwyer's final challenge and which, in the advent of the Traficant case, remained the one newspaper (followed later by its successor, *American Free Press*), which dared to tell the truth about the Traficant affair.

In the meantime, however, we will review some of Jim Traficant's more passionate "one-minute speeches" before Congress, demonstrating, perhaps best, precisely why Jim Traficant was targeted by the Justice Department in the first place. There is some hesitation in saying that any modern-day member of Congress could be a "statesman" but that word does describe Jim Traficant.

Appendix One:

A Voice for the People

Jim Traficant's
One-Minute Speeches
on the Floor of
the U.S. House of Representatives

—A selection—

Introduction . . .

During his congressional career, Jim Traficant became one of the best-known members of the House of Representatives—a body of nobodies—after millions of enthusiastic Americans saw and heard—on many of CSPAN's televised broadcasts—the short, sweet and to-the-point tirades by Traficant on controversial issues, various and sundry.

This selection—by no means comprehensive—nonetheless demonstrates the scope of Traficant's determined efforts to bring some common sense (and honesty) to the American political process, a system that clearly needs a housecleaning, as Traficant points out.

FAST TRACK SHIPS JOBS OVERSEAS
November 8, 1997

Mr. Speaker, I am opposed to fast track. When American workers are serving Mexican tomatoes and Canadian beef at Burger King and Bob Evans, something is very wrong. The American workers are not dumb.

They are fed up, they are sick and tired of unemployment compensation, sick and tired of retraining, sick and tired of promises.

They are sick and tired of politics. They are busted, disgusted, and cannot be trusted to vote for cerebral politicians who continue to ship their jobs overseas.

Now, as far as I am concerned, I listened to all this "bridge to the 21st century" business.

I say the bridge to the 21st century is turning into another bridge over the River Kwai. Beam me up. Bridge this, Mr. President.

A SCHOOL WITHOUT PRAYER
IS A SCHOOL WITHOUT GOD
November 7, 1997

Mr. Speaker, students in Alabama are skipping school protesting the fact that they are not allowed to pray. Think about it. Even though America has guns, rape, drugs, even heroin and murder in our schools, students are not allowed to pray. Unbelievable.

A school without prayer is a school without God and a nation that denies prayer is a nation that denies God; and a nation that denies God is a nation that just may welcome the devil.

Members of Congress, the Constitution may separate church and State, but the Founders never intended to separate God and the American people.

I yield back any common sense and logic we have left.

FAST TRACK IS A JOB LOSER
FOR AMERICA'S WORKERS
November 6, 1997

Mr. Speaker, to pass fast track the President said he will expand job retraining and unemployment counseling by $1.2 billion. Unbelievable. The reason is very simple: More Americans will lose their jobs on yet another fast track.

To be more specific here, fast track is a loser, a job loser for American workers. What are we retraining these workers to do? How many more pantyhose crotch closer jobs are really out there, Mr. Speaker? Beam me up.

It is time to stand up and stop this madness. American workers do not want unemployment compensation, they do not want retraining, they do not want trade adjustment assistance. They want to keep their jobs and take care of their families.

BRING SOME COMMON SENSE
TO FOREIGN RELATIONS
November 5, 1997

Mr. Speaker, see if this makes sense. America gives billions of foreign aid to Russia; Russia then takes American cash and builds new weapons; Russia then offers to sell the old weapons to Iran. America is trying to keep nuclear technology from Iran, and they buy the old weapons from Russia. Russia then asks America for more foreign aid. America—trying to keep the Marx brothers out of Russia, and I do not mean Groucho— gives Russia more foreign aid.

After all this, the State Department labels the National Council Resistance, the opposition party in Iran, fighting for democracy, trying to throw those bums out. They label them a terrorist group. Unbelievable. How dumb can Uncle Sam be? Let us tell it like it is. Those Russian nuclear scientists are not hanging around Iran to watch belly dancers. What is next? Will the Pentagon lease Tehran?

Beam me up, Mr. Speaker. With a foreign policy like this, I do not know how we still have our sovereignty.

VOTE "NO" ON NAFTA EXPANSION
November 4, 1997

Mr. Speaker, let there be no mistake. The vote today on the Caribbean Trade Partnership Act is a litmus test from the White House. They want to pass NAFTA expansion, and the President is twisting arms. In fact, the President is reminding everybody that we must build a bridge to the 21st century.

Now, if that is not enough to repave your off ramp, here is how that bridge really works. The bridge brings in Mexican tomatoes, Canadian beef, illegal immigrants, narcotics, and everything under the sun made in China and Japan. The bridge takes away American jobs, takes away American factories, destroys American families.

Beam me up. That is not a bridge the White House is selling; that is a toll road leading to a dead end for American workers. Vote `no' today on that partnership act, vote "no" on NAFTA expansion. I yield back the [good-paying] wage jobs we keep sending overseas.

WHITE HOUSE MUST ACCEPT CHANGE
IN BURDEN OF PROOF IN TAX DISPUTES
October 21, 1997

Madam Speaker, the White House is opposed to shifting the burden of proof from the taxpayer to the IRS. The White House wants to leave it alone, smack dab on the taxpayer.

The White House says it will cost too much. Unbelievable. The IRS accuses; the taxpayer must prove it. Could my colleagues imagine George Washington opposing the Bill of Rights over dollars and cents?

Shame, White House. Shame. As far as I am concerned, the White House will get the burden of proof change in a civil tax case one way or the other. They will either accept it with common sense and good logic, or they will get it as a stone cold congressional suppository.

Madam Speaker, I would tell them, "Make your choice, White House, and make our 1040. It is time to put the Bill of Rights back into the Tax Code. Audit this."

MAKE MY OVERRIDE
October 1, 1997

A spokesman said the White House will reform the IRS and any congressional bill that goes too far will be vetoed; "veto," the magic word. I expect to see Groucho's duck any day here.

Beam me up, Mr. Speaker, and it is time for Congress to take a stand. Who is kidding whom? The White House reforming the IRS would be like Barney Fife trying to reform Al Capone. My colleagues know it, I know it, and the American people know it.

Let us tell it like it is. If the President wants to carry water for the Internal Revenue Service, let him, and it is time for Congress to strap on the six-shooters and tell the President, `Make my override. Veto this.'

Let us straighten those bums out.

PASS H.R. 367 AND PUT SOME CONTROLS
ON THE INTERNAL REVENUE SERVICE
September 4, 1997

Mr. Speaker, the IRS says, "Members are picking on us." Poor, poor IRS; do I hear violins? How about a pity party? Let us tell it like it is:

When an $80,000 disagreement turns into $330,000 in penalties and fines in 3 short years, when taxpayers commit suicide, when taxpayers are told to their face that they just died, when taxpayers, in fact, are targeted for audits because they politically oppose the IRS, we are not picking on the IRS, we are telling the truth.

Mr. Speaker, the further truth is, when the IRS makes Vito Corleone look like a Boy Scout, something is very wrong.

Shame IRS, shame.

They should hide their two faces. It is time for the Congress, like the people, to be taxed off, and pass H.R. 367 and put some controls on the executive branch and the Internal Rectum Service.

FBI LEAKS TO PRESS ARE NO MISTAKE
July 31, 1997

Mr. Speaker, Louis Freeh said the FBI did not leak the name of Richard Jewell as the Atlanta bomber to the press. Who is kidding whom?

Every policeman in America knows it is a common practice of the FBI to leak information to the press.

Let us tell it like it is. The FBI is once again lying through their teeth. They lied about Ruby Ridge, they lied about Waco, they are lying about Richard Jewell. Lies, lies, lies, and they say they are mistakes.

Let there be no mistake, Congress, these are not mistakes, these are crimes and it is time for FBI criminals to be prosecuted. Stand up, Congress.

BORDER PATROLS
July 30, 1997

Mr. Speaker, due to an unfortunate shooting on the border, the Pentagon has removed our military troops from the Mexican border. That shooting must be investigated, but the simple truth is in the last 3 months seven Border Patrol agents were shot and the borders are now wide open.

And from the community where this young man was shot, a group came up to meet with me, and listen to what they said, Congress. They said they want open borders, no immigration. They oppose military troops on the border.

Of an 8-hour shift, the Border Patrol spends 6 hours in coffee shops, and their local sheriff was convicted and is in jail for smuggling 2,200 pounds of cocaine.

Beam me up. America has no drug program. We have got open borders. We have got heroin and cocaine on every street corner. Kids are dying and the White House is more concerned with politics than our children. Congress, wake up. When it is as easy to get heroin and cocaine as it is to get aspirin, there is something wrong in high places.

TIME TO LOOK AT
WORKERS' RIGHTS IN AMERICA
June 11, 1997

Mr. Speaker, since 1888, Reznor heaters were made in Mercer, PA. Yesterday, Reznor executives told their workers if you do not accept the $2.20 an hour cut, we will move the plant to Mexico; take it or leave it. Four hundred dollars a month, $5,200 a year, $15,600 in cuts over the life of a 3-year contract. Take it or leave it, workers. We will go to Mexico.

Shame, Congress. Reznor executives are holding the gun to their workers' heads. Congress is pulling the trigger all around America. Shame, Congress. How about some more NAFTA? I think it is time to take a look at the rights of American workers. I yield back any jobs that might be left.

PROVIDING HOUSING FOR
RUSSIAN SOLDIERS WHILE
AMERICANS ARE UPROOTED BY
MILITARY BASE CLOSINGS
May 22, 1997

Mr. Speaker, even though American families are being uprooted with military base closings, Uncle Sam gave millions of dollars to Russia to build housing for Russian soldiers. Now, if that is not enough to throw up your vodka, check this out.

News reports confirm that one of Russia's top generals has been arrested for taking bribes, bribed with American cash. These reports say the top Russian military officials have used American dollars to build elegant country homes, and there have hardly been any homes built for Russian soldiers.

Beam me up, Mr. Speaker.

When American veterans are losing their homes and America continues to give money to Russia, it is being used to build homes for the military elite, something is wrong.

Are we nuts here?

Is everybody inhaling in D.C.?

I say not one more dollar for these fat cat Russkie nincompoops. Let us use our money to help American military.

Mr. Speaker, I yield back the balance of any jobs and money left.

NO SUNSHINE AT FEDERAL RESERVE BOARD
May 8, 1997

Mr. Speaker, school boards, council meetings, all public meetings in America are subject to the sunshine law, except the Federal Reserve Board. The Fed says what America does not know is good for America. If that is not enough to starch your leotards, check this out:

The Federal Reserve Bank of Kansas City allowed 28 officials from China, Japan, and Europe to attend one of their meetings where they discussed monetary policy. Unbelievable.

The American people are shut out, even Congress is shut out, but the Chinese, the Japanese, and the Europeans are allowed in.

Beam me up, Mr. Speaker.

It is time for Congress to audit and investigate this bunch of internationalists setting our monetary policy that allow the Chinese and the Japanese in.

American sunshine, no way. Rising sun, welcome. The last I heard, Uncle Sam controlled the Fed, not Uncle Sucker. Let us get our job done.

CITIZENSHIP USA
May 1, 1997

Mr. Speaker, the Immigration and Naturalization Service admits that up to 180,000 criminals were improperly granted citizenship.

The INS now says we made a mistake and allowed applicants to submit copies of their own fingerprints, and the criminals submitted phony prints. Beam me up.

I say it is time to wage a real war on illegal immigration and drugs. Let us transfer some of our military troops falling out of chairs on arm rests, cashing their American paycheck in Tokyo and Frankfurt and put them on our border and stop this business.

This is a joke. This program called Citizenship USA has turned into Criminal USA. It does not take Karnak the Magnificent to figure it out.

Congress should fire those incompetent, stumbling, bumbling nincompoops at the Immigration and Naturalization Service. Print this.

I yield back the balance of all illegal immigrants.

WORLD BANK GIVING
AMERICAN DOLLARS AWAY
April 23, 1997

Mr. Speaker, the World Bank, funded by American dollars, just gave another $250 million to Russian coal miners. The problem is no one knows what happened to the first $250 million. That is right, bye-bye, $250 million.

Now, if that is not enough to massage your Chapter 11, check this out: Russian officials say the $250 million is lost. Where is the money, Mr. Speaker?

Since 1992, $7 billion of American money going to the World Bank ends up in Russia. Where is the money?

I say, while the World Bank, with American dollars, is providing jobs for Soviet and old Soviet Russian coal miners, American coal workers are getting pink slips and black lung.

Beam me up. I say somebody at the World Bank is smoking dope and they are inhaling. I think we need some common sense here. Yield back the balance of our carcinogens involved with this.

OUR VETS DESERVE THE TRUTH
April 10, 1997

Mr. Speaker, thousands of gulf war vets have complained about nerve gas problems to no avail, and after all this the CIA now admits they had warnings as early as 1984 that Iraq had stored nerve gas in their ammunition depots that were later blown up by American troops.

Unbelievable. The CIA now says they did not tell the Pentagon and it was a mistake.

Beam me up, Mr. Speaker. I do not believe the CIA, and when thousands of gulf war vets are treated like whining hypochondriacs something is very wrong. I say these vets deserve the truth and the help of Congress.

Furthermore, I say to my colleagues, if we want to balance the budget, we could save $30 billion in our intelligence budget by hiring Barney Fife, who will do a much better job and be a hell of a lot more honest.

THE JUSTICE DEPARTMENT
CANNOT POLICE ITSELF
March 20, 1997

Mr. Speaker, the Justice Department cannot police itself. At Ruby Ridge, a 14-year-old boy was shot and killed, and his mother, holding her infant child, was shot and killed, shot right between the eyes; no criminal charges.

At Waco, 83 Americans were killed, including 20 children; no criminal charges were filed.

In Chicago, a court ruled that Justice Department personnel gave sex and drugs and alcohol to a number of informants to get them to offer perjured testimony; no criminal charges were filed.

Mr. Speaker, who is kidding whom? When an unarmed 14-year-old can be shot and killed, his mother shot between the eyes, and there are no criminal charges filed, and the Justice Department says it was simply a mistake, Mr. Speaker, there is no justice in America. It is time for Congress to pass laws that will provide for independent counsel to investigate wrongdoing at the Justice Department.

COMBAT BOOTS FROM CHINA?
March 18, 1997

Mr. Speaker, last week the Pentagon denied that combat boots made in China were issued to our troops. The Pentagon said they awarded four contracts to American companies. It was impossible for that to happen.

Mr. Speaker, it is evident that the Pentagon's left foot does not know what their right foot is wearing. I have Nighthawk combat boots in my possession, made in China, that were issued to a sergeant of the Air Force Reserve.

Now, let us tell it like it is. The Pentagon has always told us in debates, if they could not buy those cheaper imports, they could not keep their costs down.

You know what I tell Congress to do? Tell the Pentagon that we can hire generals and admirals a lot cheaper from Korea, too, and we could keep the cost down.

I am asking my colleagues to join me in investigating this matter, why [Chinese-made] military combat boots were issued to our troops.

CHINA-MADE BOOTS
March 12, 1997

Mr. Speaker, it is no wonder that millions of Chinese dollars have popped up in American politics.

I mean, check it out: China alone gets $45 billion from American taxpayers in a sweetheart deal known as most-favored-nation trade status.

Now, to me, that is absolutely disgusting, with the 17 cents an hour labor wage. But if that is not enough to rip one of those false made-in-America labels on one of those Chinese imports, check this out:

The United States Air Force just issued military combat boots to our troops that were made in China. That is right. American military personnel are wearing combat boots now made in China.

Beam me up, Mr. Speaker.

What is next, Marines in Mao suits? I think it is time to take a look at what China has done and take a look at every one of these sweetheart trade deals.

I yield back the balance of all American shoe wear that has cost jobs in this country.

CHINA BUYS AMERICA
March 11, 1997

Mr. Speaker, news reports say that China tried to influence and buy last year's Federal elections, including the

Presidency. All of America is in an uproar.

Newspapers are in shock and people are calling the talk shows on the radio and saying they believe America is for sale. Can you blame them?

China gets most-favored-nation trade status but sells missiles to our enemies.

Japan keeps raping our marketplace, approaching $70 billion in surpluses, and they keep denying our products.

Mexico gets billions of dollars from us and they ship narcotics to our streets.

And now American companies overseas are advertising in the newspaper for American workers to move overseas and get a good, livable wage job.

Beam me up, Mr. Speaker. America is not for sale. I think America has already been sold, and I think Congress should start looking into it.

Sold, lock, stock, and pork barrel.

BRING OUR JOBS HOME
March 5, 1997

Mr. Speaker, jobs keep leaving America on the fast track. Wrangler Jeans is laying off 3,000 workers and moving 12 factories overseas. Apple Computer, they cut 1,500 jobs last year; they are cutting another 3,000 jobs this year. Shoemaker West is cutting 1,000 jobs, moving 3 factories overseas, and now, under WTO, Costa Rica is challenging Uncle Sam over underwear. Unbelievable.

American workers are not only losing their jobs, now they are about to lose their BVD's. It is getting so bad that in Longview, WA, a robber entered a grocery store wearing a pair of pink panties over his head. The police said they never saw anything like it. What is the surprise, Mr. Speaker? Jobs are getting so scarce in America today robbers cannot even buy pantyhose. I yield back the balance of all the lingerie and all the other problems. Beam me up, Mr. Speaker.

SUPPORT STEEL RESOLUTION
AND STAND UP FOR LEGAL TRADE
October 15, 1998

Mr. Speaker, another chapter on American steel. We have already read Chapter 11, Chapter 13, and we are about to read a stone cold Chapter 7 due to illegal trade, dumping steel in America below cost, destroying families, destroying companies, destroying jobs, destroying pensions, and nobody is doing one thing about it. We pass laws here, and the law is not being enforced. There is such a glut of steel there is a fire sale in America. America is burning. And while America burns, the administration is fiddling, doing nothing.

Today you will have an opportunity to vote on a resolution. I predict that there will be an attempt to bring a softer resolution than mine.

Today is the time to stand up for legal trade.

BAILOUT FOR RICH FAT CATS ON WALL STREET
October 13, 1998

Mr. Speaker, check this out. A bunch of rich, fat cats on Wall Street, through their hedge fund, gambled $100 billion on the Russian ruble with borrowed American money.

We can figure it out, they lost big time and the Fed had to bail them out saying if they did not, there could possibly be a depression in America.

Unbelievable, is it not? Think about it. Bailout for Russia, bailout for Japan, bailout for Mexico, bailout for rich fat cats gambling with our money, and now we are talking about an $18 billion bailout for Brazil and Russia, who are dumping steel illegally in America, destroying our economy.

Beam me up.

What is next? Foreign aid for China? I do not think Congress will wise up until Uncle Sam needs a bailout. I yield back whatever money is left.

IMF FUNDING
October 12, 1998

Mr. Speaker, the White House said, give the International Monetary Fund $18 billion more, or we will shut the government down. Take it and like it, Congress. Shut up and pass it, Congress.

Enough is enough. When will the Congress grow a backbone? What is going on here, Mr. Speaker?

I say if that is the deal, shut the government down. You know not one American will be hurt. We can retroactively take care of them. But I am not for one more penny for the international monetary slush fund.

We give them the money. They buy Chinese products with it. Foreign leaders steal it, and then they vote against us at the United Nations 90 percent of the time.

Beam me up. If we are going to flush another $18 billion down the toilet, then push the handle, Congress, and flush it in America.

I yield back the balance of anything worth flushing with the International Monetary Fund.

SOMETHING IS WRONG WITH THIS POLICY
October 7, 1998

Mr. Speaker, in America we have record trade deficits, record bankruptcies, record debt, consolidations, downsizing, more American jobs keep going overseas, a schizophrenic stock market, all symptoms of a major economic problem in America. After all this, the experts say American taxpayers must keep sending more money to the International Monetary Fund to prop up foreign countries to avert disaster. Beam me up, Mr. Speaker.

When American dollars end up in the pockets of foreign politicians who then vote against America at the United Nations, something is wrong with this policy, very wrong. I say these foreign countries do not need American taxpayer dollars. They need reform. Think about it. Mr. Speaker, I yield back what economy we have left.

AMERICA'S WORKERS
ARE SICK AND TIRED OF FAST TRACK
September 25, 1998

Mr. Speaker, American workers are sick and tired of fast track. Take today's fast track, for example, another fast track that will send more American factories, more American investment, and more American jobs overseas, this time to Central America. In return, America will get two used Ford pick-up trucks, another 50 tons of heroin and cocaine, and three baseball players ... Beam me up. Washington does not need more lobbyists and lawyers to advise Congress. I honestly believe that a proctologist is in order down here. I yield back whatever common sense is left.

AMERICAN SOVEREIGNTY
July 22, 1998

Mr. Speaker, the World Bank makes loans to communists with American dollars. The World Trade Organization regularly rips us off. The United Nations sends American troops into war. That is right. We are not sending the Peace Corps here, folks.

If that is not enough to compromise your Viagra, the United Nations has created a world court with universal authority and jurisdiction. Unbelievable. What is next, a world tax? Beam me up.

I say the Constitution of the United States should not be surrendered to a bunch of international bureaucrats who regularly rule against us, ladies and gentlemen.

Now, I do not know about you, but I did not pledge an oath to the charter of the United Nations. I pledged an oath to the Constitution of the United States and I think the Congress of the United States should put its foot down

before we become known as background music in some
doctor's office. I yield back any courage we have left.

BEAM ME UP—TEACHERS IN AMERICA
CANNOT EVEN MENTION GOD?
June 19, 1998

Mr. Speaker, Mildred Rosario, a sixth grade teacher in the
Bronx, was fired. Mildred was fired for attempting to com-
fort her students over the drowning loss of a fellow class-
mate by simply saying he was in heaven.

Mildred was fired for saying, I quote, he was in heaven.
Unbelievable.

In America teachers can pass out condoms in school.
Teachers can pass out needles. Teachers can even have
forums and discussions on devil worship. But in America
teachers cannot even mention God.

Beam me up.

A Nation that can discuss devil worship in our schools
but cannot even mention God is a Nation that has lost both
its sense of values and its sense of common sense.

Mr. Speaker, I yield back any problems we have in our
schools.

BILL OF RIGHTS APPLIES TO TAXPAYERS, TOO
June 11, 1998

Mr. Speaker, the IRS and Treasury Department want to
soften the language of the burden of proof provision in the
IRS reform bill. Let us tell it like it is. The administration
wants the accused taxpayer to remain under the gun.

Beam me up, Mr. Speaker.

If "innocent until proven guilty" is good enough for the
murderers of Jasper, Texas, good enough for Charlie Trie in
China, good enough for Bill Clinton, then innocent until
proven guilty is good enough for mom and dad, good
enough for grandma and grandpa, good enough for he and

she, you and me, good enough for my colleagues' constituent and for my constituent.

Mr. Speaker, they should keep their hands off that provision. It is the only real discipline in the reform bill. The Bill of Rights should apply to taxpayers, too. With that, I yield back any common sense left and advise the administration to come clean.

KEEP THE WORKERS AND
GET RID OF THE TOP DOGS AND FAT CATS
June 9, 1998

Mr. Speaker, last year the top dog at Bank One made $9 million. The big barker at Edison Brothers made $5 million. The kennel master at K-Mart made $6 million.

Mr. Speaker, if that is not enough to potty train a Rottweiler, the big Doberman at AT&T made $26 million, and do my colleagues know what he did? He got rid of 23,000 workers at AT&T.

Unbelievable.

Big dogs go to the penthouse, American workers go to the dog house.

I think these companies are all screwed up.

I think they should keep the workers and get rid of the fat cats at the top.

And listen to this very carefully: I say they can hire CEO's a lot cheaper in Mexico, too. Think about that.

PUT PRAYER BACK IN THE PUBLIC SCHOOL
April 29, 1998

Mr. Speaker, after the Arkansas tragedy where four students and a teacher were killed by two youngsters, the shooting death of Pennsylvania teacher John Gillette has shocked America. Experts are confused and, they say, searching for answers. The irony is these same experts, with all their degrees, have one thing in common: most of them oppose school prayer. In fact, time and time again, they have employed constitutional mumbo jumbo to kill school prayer.

They just do not get it. A school without God is a school without education. A school without God is a school without discipline.

A school without God is a school without values, ladies and gentlemen. Maybe experts will finally get the message that a school without God is a playground for the demon. The Congress should allow school prayer.

I yield back any common sense left in Washington.

REFORM THE IRS
April 28, 1998

Mr. Speaker, the IRS is trying to kill reform. They are bringing out the big guns, Congress. The Treasury Department says, and I quote, whistle blowers are lying. The IRS is really doing a good job.

Unbelievable. Tell that to the families of Alex Consul and Bruce Baron, both of whom committed suicide. Tell me, how many more Americans must commit suicide? How many more American families must be destroyed? Who is kidding whom? The tail is wagging the dog in America, and Uncle Sam is now barking the praises of the IRS.

Beam me up, Mr. Speaker.

No American should fear our government. The most important thing the Congress of the United States can do this year is reform the IRS. With that, I yield back any guts left in this great, august deliberative body.

COMMON SENSE LACKING
IN POLITICIANS IN WASHINGTON, D.C.
April 23, 1998

Mr. Speaker, in America, Communists can work in our defense plants, illegal immigrants who jump the fence can get citizenship, there are law libraries for mass murderers; some want free condoms for school children, and some now want free needles for drug addicts. Think about it. Free condoms, free needles, but in America, no school prayer.

Is it any wonder the streets of America are full of narcotics and blood?

The founders believed that a Nation without prayer would be a Nation without God. I agree. The Congress should pass school prayer.

I yield back the balance of any common sense left in any of the politicians in Washington, D.C.

EXPANDING NAFTA TO CENTRAL AMERICA
April 21, 1998

Mr. Speaker, somebody is inhaling. Since NAFTA, American TVs and typewriters are made in Mexico; American telephones are made in Singapore; computers are made in China and Japan. And after all this, the White House wants to expand this NAFTA madness to all of Central America.

Now, here is how I predict it will work. Central America will get jobs and investment. Uncle Sam will get a pink slip, training voucher, and two free lunches to Taco Bell. Beam me up. This is not free trade. This is a joke, a dirty joke on American workers.

I yield back another record trade deficit and 1.4 million American workers who filed individual bankruptcy in America last year, another record I might add. Think about it.

THE CONSTITUTION
NEVER INTENDED TO BAN SCHOOL PRAYER
March 30, 1998

Mr. Speaker, America is still in shock. Two boys, age 11 and 13, gunned down four young students in a middle school in Arkansas, and the experts are asking what happened to parents? What happened to values? What happened to our schools?

Schools are overrun with drugs, violence, guns, rape, murder, and now even mass murder. It seems America's schools have everything, Congress, everything except prayer. Maybe the so-called experts might finally realize that a nation that denies God in our schools is a nation that encourages the devil in our schools. The Constitution never, never intended to ban school prayer and never intended to separate God and the American people. Think about it.

SECURING BORDERS FOR AMERICAN PEOPLE
March 26, 1998

Mr. Speaker, a classified U.S. Government report says that Mexico's military is allowing massive shipments of narcotics into America. Wow, what a surprise. Barney Fife even knows that, folks. Let us tell it like it is.

Mexico is the biggest drug pusher in the world, and Uncle Sam is the world's biggest junkie. Shame, Congress. It is time to stop this narcotic madness.

Number one, Congress should absolutely repeal NAFTA; and number two, if Congress can ensure the securing of borders in Bosnia, Western Europe, the Mideast, and Korea, then, by God, Congress should be able to secure the borders for the American people.

Think about that. This narcotics business is not hard to figure out.

I yield back all the balance of overdoses in our cities throughout the country.

USE AMERICAN TROOPS
TO GUARD AMERICAN BORDER
February 11, 1998

Mr. Speaker, the Immigration and Naturalization Service in some of their offices has error rates as high as 99 percent in reviewing applications, according to a recent study. In addition, 13,000 immigrants bought citizenship with illegal payoffs and bribes.

Now, if that is not enough to compromise your disgust, check this out: The INS says keep the military off the borders, Congress.

Unbelievable.

These same bungling, incompetent nincompoops who have allowed heroin and cocaine to be easier to get than aspirin, who have our borders overrun with illegal immigrants, now want the border all to themselves.

Beam me up. The American people want Congress to secure our borders.

Let me say this, Congress:

If American troops can guard borders for the United Nations all over the world, American troops can guard the American border at home for the American people.

I think we should investigate those bungling nincompoops at the INS.

I yield back the one percent positive rate they have.

TIME TO ABOLISH INCOME TAXES
November 10, 1999

Mr. Speaker, in America, the government takes the people's money and distributes it.

That sounds like communism to me. I think it is time to throw out income taxes.

No more forms, no more audits, no more IRS. Think about it.

I am going to quote now Reverend Jim Ford. He says, think about this: The IRS does not even send us a thank you for voluntarily paying our income taxes.

Beam me up.

It is time to abolish income taxes, abolish the IRS, and pass a flat 15 percent national sales tax.

CRIMINALS HAVE MORE RIGHTS
THAN LAW-ABIDING CITIZENS
November 09, 1999

Mr. Speaker, a Minnesota factory worker said, enough is enough. His cabin was ripped off three times. His neighbors' cabins continue to be ripped off. The police said they could do nothing. So Lenny Miller booby-trapped his cabin and busted the burglar red-handed. And guess what? Some bust. Lenny Miller is going to jail with a $12,000 fine. And the burglar is getting free healthcare.

Beam me up.

Something is wrong, Mr. Speaker, when Americans cannot protect their own property and when criminals have more rights than law-abiding citizens.

There is one bright side. I yield back the fact that in Wisconsin there will not be many cabins ripped off this year thanks to Lenny Miller.

ENFORCE EXISTING GUN LAWS;
DO NOT CODDLE GUN VIOLATORS
November 02, 1999

Madam Speaker, the White House wants more gun control. Janet Reno wants more gun control. But something just does not add up, Madam Speaker.

In the last 5 years, prosecution of gun violators dropped 50 percent. Gun violators serve 25 percent less time in jail, and many pardons were granted for gun violators.

Now think about it.

Fewer prosecutions, early releases, pardons, but the White House wants more gun control. Beam me up, Madam Speaker. America does not need more gun control. America needs the White House to enforce the gun laws we already have. I yield back all the coddling of these gun violators by this administration.

IRS OUT OF CONTROL
October 26, 1999
America's income tax is not only un-American, it is socialism at its best.

It promotes dependency, penalizes achievement, kills jobs, kills investment, and subsidizes illegitimacy. It is out of control, Members of Congress.

If that is not enough to tax your Social Security from cradle to the grave they keep busting our balsam and taxing us even when we die.

Beam me up here, Mr. Speaker.

I say it is time to literally abolish both the IRS and the progressive un-American socialistic income tax.

Audit this.

I yield back the socialism of our income tax program.

WACO STILL A BURNING QUESTION
October 25, 1999
Mr. Speaker, after 6 years, Waco is still burning.

These fires will not stop until our government tells the truth. [Some] Ninety Americans killed, and nobody, nobody has been held accountable to this date, even though the government used deadly gas, used a [tank], and could have arrested David Koresh any morning out jogging.

Now, despite government denial, they find a high caliber shell casing near a position stand of an FBI sniper.

Beam me up, Mr. Speaker.

One can fool some of the people some of the time, but one cannot fool all of the people all of the time.

The government is lying about Waco.

I yield back the fact that the Justice Department, by the way, investigates themselves.

PROGRESSIVE INCOME TAX SOCIALISM
September 24, 1999

Mr. Speaker, in 1848, Karl Marx said a progressive income tax is needed to transfer wealth and power to the state. Thus, Marx's Communist Manifesto had as its major economic tenet a progressive income tax.

Think about it, 1848, Karl Marx, Communism.

Now, if that is not enough to tax our history, 1999, United States of America, progressive income tax socialism. Stone cold socialism.

I say it is time to replace the progressive income tax with a national retail sales tax, and it is time to abolish the IRS, my colleagues.

I yield back all the rules, regulations, fear, and intimidation of our current system.

NEW WORLD BILL COLLECTORS
September 22, 1999

Mr. Speaker, the U.N. says we owe them a billion dollars and if we do not pay we will lose our vote.

The U.N. also said they accepted three new member countries. All three are smaller than the hometowns of my colleagues. One has 8,000 people.

Now, if that is not enough to tax our peacekeeping, check this out. These three countries will have three votes. We will still have one vote.

Beam me up, Mr. Speaker.

The truth is the United Nations owes Uncle Sam $6 billion for saving their international assets year in and year out.

I say it is time for Congress to tell these New World bill collectors to shove their debt up their charter.

Think about that.

I yield back the big vote we will lose at the United Nations.

FEAR AND INTIMIDATION
HAVE NO PLACE IN AMERICAN GOVERNMENT
September 15, 1999

Mr. Speaker, last year under oath the IRS admitted in testimony "We use fear and intimidation to make Americans pay their taxes." That is right, fear.

It is not just the IRS. Take Waco. Waco is about a group of Americans, good, bad, or indifferent, who defied the government.

They stood up to the government and the government crushed them. The government crushed them, to send a message. What was that message, Mr. Speaker? They had better fear the government.

Beam me up, Mr. Speaker.

Fear is an ugly four-letter word. It has no place in American government.

I yield back all the fear and intimidation of our government agencies.

A WHOLE NEW POLICY ON TERRORISM:
IF TERRORISTS APOLOGIZE, THEY ARE SET FREE
September 9, 1999

Madam Speaker, 12 terrorists from Puerto Rico who are responsible for 130 bombings in America, killing 6 Americans and wounding many more have been pardoned by the President.

Now, if that is not enough to get away with murder, check this out: to get the pardon, the terrorists had to promise to give up violence. Unbelievable, Madam Speaker.

A whole new policy on terrorism in America. If terrorists apologize, they are set free. Beam me up, Madam Speaker.

An America that pardons terrorists is an America that invites more terrorism.

I yield back the pain and suffering of their victims and their families.

WACO: THE FBI LIED
AND THE ATTORNEY GENERAL LIED
September 8, 1999

Madam Speaker, in 1993, 86 civilians were killed in Waco, Texas. Twenty-four of them were innocent children. Most of them burned to death. Until this day, no one knows the truth about Waco, and the reason is quite clear.

The FBI lied and the Attorney General of the United States lied. They lied and they covered it up. And after all of these lies, no one, nobody, has been held accountable for the massacre at Waco.

Beam me up, Mr. Speaker; an America that turns its back on Waco is an America that turns its back on freedom and justice. An independent investigation is absolutely warranted to solve this cover-up and get to the truth.

I yield back all the lies at the Justice Department.

COVER-UP IN WACO, TEXAS
August 4, 1999

Mr. Speaker, over 80 Americans were killed at Waco, many of them women and children, actually burned to death, and the Texas Rangers have now uncovered new evidence that said the Federal Government covered up the truth and lied about Waco. Check it out. A recent memo says, Federal agents had a friendly meeting with Koresh just 9 days before the assault, yet Federal agents testified in court, and I quote, they said, they could not lure Koresh from the compound and were forced to engage in the assault.

Unbelievable. The Justice Department is lying through their teeth. Mr. Speaker, 700 Federal agents, tanks, and rocket power attacked American civilians, 80 of them killed, many of them women and children, burned to death, and nobody did anything about it. Nobody. It is time for an independent investigation into the FBI, the Justice Department, and the cover-up in Waco, Texas.

AMERICAN BORDERS WIDE OPEN
WHILE GUARDING BOSNIA AND KOSOVO
July 14, 1999

Mr. Speaker, all heroin and cocaine comes across our borders, and everyone agrees that heroin and cocaine cause most of the crime, murder, and medical bills in America. And Congress does nothing.

While American soldiers are guarding the borders of Bosnia and Kosovo, American borders are wide open. And Congress does nothing.

Beam me up, Mr. Speaker.

A Nation without secure borders is a Nation without security. A Congress that turns its back on our borders is a Congress that invites disaster.

I yield back the stupid un-American policies.

OUR COUNTRY'S
UNBELIEVABLE POLICY ON STEEL
July 13, 1999

Mr. Speaker, after World War II we gave tours of our steel mills to Japan and Germany.

We let them take pictures. We gave them blueprints. We even gave them foreign aid so they could build their own steel mills.

Today Japan and Germany have steel mills. America has photographs.

If that is not enough to tarnish our stainless, Japan and Europe at this very moment keep dumping illegal steel into America while in Pittsburgh, the once steel capital of the world, they just demolished another steel mill.

Beam me up.

This policy on steel is not only unbelievable, it is stupid.

I believe, Mr. Speaker, we could do with less think tanks and styrofoam and a few more factories and steel.

PRESIDENTIAL ELECTION DEBATES
SHOULD INCLUDE ALL VIABLE CANDIDATES
July 1, 1999

Mr. Speaker, last November polls in Minnesota said it was a two-man race for governor. Beam me up.

Who were they polling? Bullwinkle? Jesse Ventura, the third candidate, actually won due to the debates and quite frankly he is a breath of fresh air in our country.

That is the reason, another reason, why I have reintroduced my bill that would require that all presidential debates must include every candidate that has a mathematical chance of winning.

They qualify on enough State ballots. They qualify for matching funds. They give the American people a choice, and they make the two major party candidates tell us what they really feel.

I yield back Bullwinkle, and I yield back the fact that the Federal Election Commission can do this without my bill.

GUNS PREVENT MORE CRIME
THAN ANYTHING ELSE
June 16, 1999

Mr. Speaker, I voted for the Brady bill. I voted to ban certain semiautomatic weapons.

I honestly tried to help.

But enough is enough. Guns are a two-edge sword, dangerous for sure, but guns prevent more crime than anything else in America, and no one is saying it.

Mr. Speaker, armed robbers just do not fear the welcome wagon, and all the policemen in the world, and I used to be one, may never get there in time.

I say be careful, Congress. Certainly guns are a symptom of great problems in America. But guns are not the root causation of all these problems in America.

IT IS TIME TO ABOLISH OUR TAX CODE
AND THROW THE IRS OUT WITH IT
April 15, 1999

Madam Speaker, our Tax Code penalizes achievement and rewards dependence. It subsidizes illegitimacy. It kills investment. It kills jobs. It destroys our exports and sales and subsidizes our imports.

Beam me up, Madam Speaker. In a nutshell, our Tax Code sucks. It is time to abolish it and throw the IRS out with it and give serious consideration to a national retail sales tax. It is time to tell the IRS, tax this.

I yield back the $850 charge of compliance for every man, woman and child in America for this complex Tax Code we have in place.

FDA MISGUIDED ON PRIORITIES
February 9, 1999

Mr. Speaker, the Food and Drug Administration has approved a new-state-of-the-art antidepressant for dogs. The FDA says "American canines are suffering from anxiety."

Think about it, no barking beagles, no more whining weimaraners, no more defecating Dobermans.

Meanwhile, the FDA continues to deny approval for certain cancer-treating drugs to help mom and dad.

Beam me up.

It is evident that the FDA has gone to the dogs. What is next, Viagra for felines?

I yield back all the misguided priorities of the Food and Drug Administration.

ACCIDENTAL HOSPITAL DEATHS ARE
HIGHER THAN ACCIDENTAL GUN DEATHS
July 26, 2000

Mr. Speaker, accidental deaths caused by doctors and hospitals in America reached 120,000 per year. Meanwhile, gun deaths have dropped 35 percent. In fact, accidental gun deaths dropped to 1,500 last year.

Think about it. We have got hospitals slicing and dicing American people like Freddie Kruger, and Congress is passing more gun laws. Beam me up. There is something wrong in America when one is 80 times more likely to be killed by a doctor than Smith & Wesson. Think about it, 80 to 1.

Maybe we need a gun in surgery.

I yield back the fact that the second amendment was not written to cover just duck hunters.

POLITICAL CORRECTNESS
RULES AT SUPREME COURT
June 20, 2000

The Supreme Court says pornography is okay and it is okay to burn the flag, that Communists can work in our defense plants, that it is okay to teach witchcraft in our schools and that it is okay for our students to write papers about the devil.

But the Supreme Court says it is illegal to write papers about Jesus, it is illegal to pray in school, and now the Supreme Court says it is even illegal to pray before a football game.

Beam me up.

I thought the founders intended to create a Supreme Court, not the Supreme Being. Think about that statement.

I yield back a Supreme Court that is so politically correct they are downright stupid, so stupid they could throw themselves at the ground and miss.

WHO IS LYING ABOUT WACO?
May 17, 2000

Mr. Speaker, who is lying about Waco? Scientist Carl Ghigliotti said the FBI lied, that they did fire automatic weapons into the burning building. But Vector Data Systems of England said the FBI did not lie. Two scientific groups totally disagree.

But something stinks. Vector gets hundreds of millions of dollars in contracts from the FBI. Carl Ghigliotti was just found dead. To boot, FBI audio tapes of the burning building are now lost. To boot, FBI autopsy reports confiscated of victims are now missing.

Beam me up, Mr. Speaker. This is not a Justice Department. This is a cover-up. We need an investigation. Congress should pass H.R. 4105 and put some oversight on what is developing into a police state in America.

CALLING FOR A FULL INVESTIGATION
INTO THE DEATH OF CARL GHIGLIOTTI
May 9, 2000

Mr. Speaker, Carl Ghigliotti, the 42-year-old scientist who investigated the Waco massacre, whose body has been missing for 2 weeks, was found dead. Ghigliotti is the man who flat out said, "The FBI is lying about Waco. The FBI did fire automatic weapons into the burning building."

Something is wrong here, Mr. Speaker. Records now show the FBI lodged an alleged or false child abuse charge against the Davidians.

The FBI denied, then admitted, using tear gas. The FBI confiscated, then supposedly lost, vital autopsy evidence that would prove what happened in Waco.

Beam me up.

We have developed a stone cold police state in America, believe me, from Waco, Ruby Ridge, to Miami, Florida.

Every American knows it, no one is doing anything about it. There must be a full investigation into the death of Carl Ghigliotti.

I yield back the need to pass some oversight on this Justice Department and pass my bill, H.R. 4105.

THE SELL-OUT OF AMERICA
May 2, 2001

Mr. Speaker, the Great Lakes are now open. The first foreign ship to dock in Cleveland, Ohio, carried 10,000 tons of steel from Russia.

While mills are closing in Cleveland, Youngstown, and Pittsburgh, steel mills are closing all over America. Ten thousand tons of illegally dumped steel just came in to America. Unbelievable. Think about it. It is getting so bad the Army almost bought, without Congress' interference, black berets for the Army from China. Beam me up.

If our trade program is so good, why does Europe not do it? Why does Japan not do it? Why does China not do it?

I think it is time to put things in order in America, my colleagues. Enough is enough. I yield back the sell-out of America, wholesale, to Communist dictators, and the loss of jobs to these socialist, communist countries.

PASS FLAT SALES TAX AND ABOLISH IRS
March 27, 2001

Mr. Speaker, in 1998, Congress reformed the IRS and included two of my provisions. The first transferred the burden of proof from the taxpayer to the IRS; the second required judicial consent before the IRS could seize our property, and the results are now staggering. Property seizures dropped from 10,037 to 161 in the entire country.

The IRS had a license to steal, and they were stealing 10,000 properties a year.

And if that is not enough to tax our gallbladders, the IRS is now complaining the new law is too tough. Beam me up here. It is time to tell these crybaby IRS thieves that we are going to pass a 15 percent flat sales tax and abolish them altogether. I yield back what should be the next endangered species in the United States of America:

The Internal Rectal Service.

THE IRS CAN NOW RAID CHURCHES
February 28, 2001

Mr. Speaker, imagine a raid by 150 policemen. Was it a mob bust in Russia? No.

Was it a drug warehouse in China? No.

It was a church in Indianapolis. That is right. The Internal Revenue Service raided a Baptist church seizing the pastor, and, in fact, removing the pastor by force. Unbelievable.

Now, everyone knows there is two sides to every story. Think about it. In America, you cannot pray in school, but now, the IRS can raid churches. Beam me up. America is going to hell in a hand basket.

I yield back the Gestapo attitude that just keeps growing in our Federal Government.*

---

*__Editorial Note:__ Although many of Congressman Traficant's one-minute speeches published here perhaps deserve a footnote, this last speech reprinted—although there were many more to come during Traficant's last year and half in Congress—bears special mention. Here Traficant is referring to the IRS and Justice Department raid on the Indianapolis Baptist Temple, one of the first actions by the new George W. Bush administration upon assuming office. The very attorney general (John Ashcroft) who came into office with the support of Christian churches and organizations promptly used his police power to attempt to destroy an independent church that dared to stand against federal encroachment upon the First Amendment guarantees of separation of church and state. Thus, should it surprise anyone that, ultimately, Jim Traficant himself would also fall victim to the intrigues of this same Justice Department? Again, a lesson to be learned for those Americans who still—inexplicably—place trust in "their" government.

The Budd Dwyer Affair:
A Retrospective

Pennsylvania State Treasurer R. Budd Dwyer (right) was a figure beloved by all who knew him and his integrity was never questioned until his erstwhile friend and fellow Republican—former Pennsylvania Governor Dick Thornburgh (left)—turned against him and utilized his connections in the Justice Department and the FBI to orchestrate trumped-up corruption charges against Dwyer. Following his conviction, Dwyer committed public suicide, calling for the mass media to expose the conspiracy to destroy him. The press chose to look the other way.

The Budd Dwyer Affair:
How the Justice Department
Destroyed a Decent and Honorable Man

Here's the story behind the story of the shocking public suicide of Pennsylvania State Treasurer R. Budd Dwyer in Harrisburg, the state capital, on January 22, 1987. The circumstances of Dwyer's suicide—and the events that preceded it—provide a startling inside view of the massive corruption and political intrigue that has been a hallmark of modern "justice" at the hands of the U.S. Department of Justice and the FBI exemplified all too clearly once again in later years by those same forces when they set up and took down Congressman Jim Traficant.

What follows is the account of the Dwyer affair as it was first described in the pages of the weekly *Spotlight* newspaper following Dwyer's untimely death. No other newspaper in America—with the exception of *American Free Press* (now published on Capitol Hill in Washington)—has ever dared to tell the story that Dwyer hoped that the "responsible" media would tell.

In the weeks following Budd Dwyer's suicide, circulating throughout political circles in Pennsylvania (particularly within Republican ranks) were copies of an explosive document that should have exposed what many called "the biggest political railroad job in years."

The document—if widely publicized—threatened to derail the unannounced, but very evident, national ambitions of a former Republican governor of Pennsylvania, Dick Thornburgh, and it also pointed the way toward a much-needed major investigation of the U.S. Justice Department.

The document in question was the typewritten 21-page statement that Pennsylvania's popular and respected state treasurer, R. Budd Dwyer, released at a press conference on

the morning of January 22. The assembled members of the
press expected Dwyer to resign his post, following his conviction on bribery charges.

Instead, Dwyer concluded his conference by drawing a
.357 Magnum revolver, placing the barrel in his mouth and
killing himself.

The treasurer hoped his dramatic death would result in
a media investigation of how he was set up by his political
opponents, including his fellow Republican, former Gov.
Dick Thornburgh, and that the media would expose the tactics used by a Justice Department prosecutor, James West (a
longtime Thornburgh associate), to engineer his conviction.
Dwyer believed that if he, a powerful elected official in one
of the largest states in the union, could be unjustly prosecuted, convicted and eventually sentenced to prison, so,
too, could thousands of other innocent people.

The irony, however, is that the media instead concen-
trated its attention on sensationalizing Dwyer's suicide.
Television footage of Dwyer's death was shown again and
again. Indelicate photographs of his final moments were
published in hundreds, if not thousands, of newspapers
coast to coast and in Europe as well.

The Washington Post, which is almost universally hailed
as America's political newspaper of record, outdid itself. The
Establishment newspaper published one particularly graph-
ic photo of Dwyer that appears to have been published
nowhere else.

The *Post*, like virtually all of the major media, told its
readers that Dwyer had read a "rambling" statement before
he took his life. Never once did the *Post* explain the substance of Dwyer's statement, other than to note that the
treasurer had (as he had been doing the past two years) proclaimed his innocence of the charges upon which he had
been convicted.

The Spotlight obtained a copy of Dwyer's statement,

among other materials he prepared before his suicide. The statement was not, by any stretch of imagination, "rambling."

Instead, it was a clear, thoughtful, totally rational, concisely written exposition of Dwyer's side of the story. The statement was a powerful indictment of certain forces in the Pennsylvania Republican and Democratic parties and in the U.S. Justice Department, working in league with a host of corrupt businessmen to engineer the political assassination of R. Budd Dwyer.

Dwyer joined a long list of innocent men and women unjustly prosecuted by the Justice Department, among them a number of respected public officials including former Reps. George V. Hansen (R-Idaho) and John Dowdy (D-Texas), most of whom—like Dwyer—committed the sole crime of taking on the political Establishment.

His suicide came on the heels of a widely publicized two-and-a-half year controversy arising from what was known in the Keystone State as the "CTA scandal."

"CTA" stood for "Computer Technology Associates Ltd.," a California firm, which allegedly offered Dwyer a $300,000 kickback in return for Dwyer, as Pennsylvania state treasurer, awarding it a $4.6-million no-bid contract. The contract was for the work of assisting Pennsylvania public schools in recovering some $40 million in Social Security taxes improperly withheld from school employees.

Dwyer was convicted on December 18, 1986 for his alleged role in the conspiracy, and on January 22, 1987 he shot himself.

CTA was the brainchild of John Torquato. Torquato was originally from Johnstown, Pennsylvania and was the son of John Torquato who was for 37 years the Democratic Party boss in Cambria County, in west-central Pennsylvania. The elder Torquato was convicted for extortion in the mid-1970s, following an investigation by the Justice Department.

It was none other than R. Budd Dwyer, then a state senator, who made the initial inquiries that launched the investigation that ended in Torquato senior's conviction. One Pennsylvania Republican leader described the younger Torquato's subsequent testimony against Dwyer as "little John's revenge."

In late 1983 the younger Torquato, accompanied by attorney William T. Smith, began approaching Pennsylvania state lawmakers with proposals regarding CTA's ability to assist the state of Pennsylvania in recovering the lost Social Security funds. Smith, who subsequently became a key witness against Dwyer, was then the chairman of the Republican Party of Dauphin County, Pennsylvania (which surrounds the capital city of Harrisburg).

On February 27, 1984 Torquato and Smith met with Dwyer and his top aides to discuss possible legislation clearing the way for a contract between CTA and the Pennsylvania state Treasury Department. (The legislation was ultimately approved and subsequently signed into law by then-Gov. Dick Thornburgh.)

On March 2, 1984 Torquato and Smith again met with Dwyer. It is at this point, Torquato later claimed, that Smith offered Dwyer $300,000 in return for Dwyer's awarding the Treasury Department contract to CTA.

Smith claimed that it was Torquato who raised the topic of money. Whatever the case, their stories conflicted.

Dwyer said that absolutely no money was discussed.

When Smith was subsequently tried on charges of offering Dwyer a bribe, Dwyer served as a defense witness on Smith's behalf, asserting that no such bribe had ever been offered.

Smith told his own attorney, John Rogers Carroll, and Dwyer's attorney, Paul Killion, that no bribe was ever offered to Dwyer. Smith said, however, that he had, in fact, told Torquato that a bribe had been offered. His motive in telling Torquato this falsehood, Smith said, was to end

Torquato's constant insistence that he, Smith, offered a bribe to Dwyer.

Smith noted that Torquato had a habit of offering bribes in order to win contracts for CTA, and that he, Smith, had told Torquato that a bribe had been offered to Dwyer in the hope that this would end Torquato's constant carping.

"Smith walked in fear of John Torquato," one source close to the case told *The Spotlight*, "and would do anything to keep Torquato off his back. That including creating a phony story about offering a bribe to Dwyer. Torquato, as a result, probably actually believed that Dwyer had agreed to accept a bribe."

Killion, Dwyer's attorney, expressed doubt that the bribe offer was ever made.

"Dwyer wasn't one of the guys. He wasn't street-smart. Someone else's antenna would have gone up [in such a conversation]. Budd was too open and not defensive about protecting himself. He was just not attuned to something that could have a double meaning," Killion said after Dwyer's suicide.

No money ever actually changed hands, but after Smith was convicted and sentenced to jail and a fine of $63,000, U.S. Attorney James West threatened to indict Smith's wife (who was also his law partner and allegedly involved in the bribery conspiracy) unless Smith cooperated in the prosecution of Dwyer.

(Referring to West's deal with Smith, Dwyer commented: "That wasn't even a plea bargain. It was just an outrageous deal that is legal under our current 'justice' system.")

It was at this point that Smith, under the gun, changed his story and in testimony at Dwyer's trial, claimed that he, indeed, offered Dwyer a bribe and that Dwyer had agreed to accept it. On the witness stand during the Dwyer trial, Smith broke down and began sobbing, declaring, "I'd do anything to protect my wife."

Shortly after giving this testimony, Smith suffered a near-fatal heart attack, requiring emergency surgery. This, Dwyer said, "dramatized the weight of Smith's guilty conscience."

Smith's admission that he would "do anything" (presumably even changing his story and perjuring himself to satisfy the Justice Department) to protect his wife from prosecution, courtroom observers believed, appeared to clinch the case in Dwyer's behalf. Dwyer's attorney believed then, that no defense was necessary for his client, and offered none. But Dwyer was nonetheless convicted.

Dwyer signed the contract with CTA on May 10, 1984. It was during this period that the office of Democratic state auditor general Al Benedict launched an investigation of the CTA contract following "leaks" which hinted that there were bribery attempts being carried out in the course of the contract negotiations. Benedict, completing his second term in office, was, by this time, the Democratic Party's candidate challenging Dwyer's re-election bid in the upcoming general election.

Benedict himself had been under investigation (in regard to another matter) and his top aide had been convicted and sent to prison for criminal activities that many people believed that Benedict should have been aware of.

During the subsequent campaign, the race between Dwyer and Benedict began to grow increasingly bitter as Benedict hammered away at Dwyer in the wake of growing controversy over the CTA scandal. Benedict sought to shift the public's attention from his own tarnished political image and onto Dwyer's own imbroglio.

On June 25, 1984 Benedict's office turned the results of its own investigation of the CTA case over to the Federal Bureau of Investigation. On July 6 the FBI searched Torquato's CTA office in California, seizing computer printouts which identified Dwyer as the alleged eventual recipient of a $300,000 bribe.

As noted previously, Torquato, based upon William Smith's false previous claims, no doubt legitimately believed that Dwyer had agreed to accept a bribe. As a consequence Torquato made note of this in his computer records.

After becoming aware of the FBI investigation, Dwyer canceled the contract with CTA on July 13. Ten days later a federal grand jury was convened in Harrisburg to investigate the affair.

In November of 1984 Torquato, Smith, and Judy Ellis (Torquato's girlfriend and an officer of CTA) and Alan Stoneman, another CTA official, pleaded not guilty to an assortment of charges arising from the CTA scandal. But Torquato reversed himself and in a plea bargain deal with U.S. Attorney James West agreed to plead guilty in return for a substantially reduced sentence. Thus, Torquato, despite his central role as the mastermind of the CTA conspiracy, became West's key witness against his associate Smith and ultimately against Dwyer.

On May 13, 1986, nearly a year and a half later, a federal grand jury indicted Dwyer for his alleged role in the conspiracy. Dwyer himself resisted the opportunity to enter into a plea bargain which would have reduced the charges against him to one unspecified count. He would have then faced a five-year prison term instead of the 55-year prison sentence he finally faced.

But Dwyer insisted on pleading not guilty and on December 18, 1986, after a four-week trial, he was convicted. Dwyer continued to maintain his innocence. He believed that in the course of a full-fledged and fairly conducted trial he could clear his name and win an acquittal. But this was not to be so.

In his statement issued just before his suicide, Dwyer outlined, in frightening detail, how, in his judgment, U.S. Attorney James West and his Justice Department had deliberately orchestrated his conviction.

The reason for this, according to Dwyer, was because the
U.S. attorney who was prosecuting the case, James West, was
a longtime political associate of then-Gov. Dick Thornburgh
(a former high-ranking Justice Department official) who
had, Dwyer said, vowed to "get" him.

In February of 1984 Dwyer had refused to pay a travel
voucher presented by the governor's wife Ginny, following
a trip to Europe. Mrs. Thornburgh wanted her personal trip
reimbursed by the taxpayers of Pennsylvania. But Dwyer
refused. It was at this time, according to Dwyer, that
Thornburgh told a number of people that he would "get"
Dwyer. According to Dwyer, Thornburgh was soon beginning to Dwyer as "the fat fuck."

Shortly thereafter, according to Dwyer, he upset the governor again. A reporter for the *Philadelphia Inquirer* had
brought to Dwyer's attention the fact that Thornburgh was
using a state police security detail to chauffeur his sons back
and forth from a private school in New England. Dwyer
questioned this expenditure of taxpayers' money for the
personal benefit of the Thornburgh family.

Dwyer noted in his final statement that the governor and
his staff made a number of attempts to embarrass him politically, but that none of these attempts was successful.

"And then," said Dwyer, "the CTA investigation by the
U.S. attorney fell into [Thornburgh's] lap and they had the
vehicle that if steered skillfully would really 'get' me."

Dwyer quoted one Thornburgh ally as saying "The fat
fuck is doing to get it now."

Dwyer faulted the major media for failing to "expose the
close connection between Thornburgh and acting U.S.
Attorney James West," who prosecuted Dwyer. From
Dwyer's statement:

> It is a matter of public record that West's first job
> after his judicial clerkship was to be hired by then-

U.S. Attorney Dick Thornburgh as an assistant U.S. Attorney in the Western District of Pennsylvania in August of 1974. It is also public information that West's second job was to be hired by then-Governor Thornburgh as a Pennsylvania deputy attorney general on April 2, 1979.

Then after President Reagan took office in 1981, the Thornburgh group tried to take over the U.S. attorney's office for the Middle District of Pennsylvania by having another two-time Thornburgh appointee, Henry Barr, appointed . . . U.S. attorney. However, Barr was not recommended by the Merit Selection Committee, and David Dart Queen was nominated and confirmed as the U.S. attorney.

But assistant U.S. attorneys do not have to go through the Merit Selection Committee process, and in July of 1982 the Thornburgh group succeeded in having none other than James "Jimmy" West named first assistant U.S. attorney for the Middle District of Pennsylvania with his office right across Capitol Park from Thornburgh's office.

It was well known in campaign circles in the fall of 1984 that Governor Thornburgh and his top staff members were desperately trying to have U.S. Attorney Queen's announcement of the first CTA indictments delayed until after the November 6 general election. They knew, through West, that [Republican State Attorney General] LeRoy Zimmerman's name would be prominently mentioned in the [CTA scandal] for the first time.

They were afraid that a pre-election announcement would cause Zimmerman's defeat and that [Democratic candidate] Allen Ertel as attorney general could conduct an investigation of the Thornburgh administration's sweetheart . . . legal

contracts. [Thornburgh defeated Ertel in the 1982
gubernatorial race, just two years previously, following a bitter campaign.—Ed.]

Queen went ahead with his announcement on
October 23, 1984 and Zimmerman almost lost the
election. The effort to remove Queen as U.S. attorney
began immediately because he could not be controlled. After a heavy political battle, Queen was
"promoted" to a position in the U.S. Treasury
Department.

When Queen departed for Washington in January
of 1985, James West was named as the acting U.S.
attorney by a 4-2 vote of the federal judges in the
Middle District, and Governor Thornburgh had his
lackey in charge of the CTA investigation, and, as we
now know, my fate was sealed.

(Dwyer also alleged in his final statement that then-state
Republican Chairman Bob Asher [who ultimately became
Dwyer's co-defendant in the bribery trial] interfered with
Thornburgh's efforts to use Republican State Committee
funds to promote Thornburgh for a spot on the 1988
Republican ticket. Asher, convicted with Dwyer, also faced
a 55-year prison sentence, but in the wake of Dwyer's suicide, federal district Judge Malcolm Muir levied only a one-
year-and-one-day sentence and also a substantial fine.)

"You now know," said Dwyer, "in case you've ever won-
dered, why, out of all the politicians' names on Torquato's
[records] and all the testimony about bribes, gifts, favors and
contributions to politicians from Smith and Torquato, the
only two politicians to be indicted and found guilty are
Budd Dwyer and Bob Asher."

According to Dwyer, "one of the major unpublished reasons Thornburgh did not run against Sen. Arlen Specter (in
the 1986 GOP Senate primary) is that Thornburgh's key

staffer was told by Specter's key staffer that if Thornburgh ran his role in the CTA affair would be a major issue in the campaign."

In his final statement Dwyer outlined, in detail, a number of ways in which, in his view, U.S. Attorney West and the Justice Department manipulated the course of events in order to ensure Dwyer's conviction.

Dwyer took particular issue with the decision to try the case in Williamsport in north-central Pennsylvania, rather than in Harrisburg, where the events of the case had taken place and where most of the principals involved lived and worked.

Dwyer said that the purpose of conducting the trial in Williamsport was to ensure that a jury pool would be selected that would have difficulty digesting the complex series of events involved in the CTA case. "Demographics indicated," said Dwyer, "that the Williamsport federal jury pool is the most uneducated in the state."

"Even so, West used several preemptory challenges to eliminate educated people from the jury. [In the end, as a result of West's efforts] there were [only] two college-educated jurors, one [a] music major and the other a psychologist, who West had originally knocked off [of the jury] but who he permitted to serve after the defense and news media complained about his tactics."

(When this writer questioned West about Dwyer's charges regarding the jury, West went so far as to point out that that one of the jurors was a psychologist. He failed to mention, however, that he, West, had tried to have that juror removed from hearing the case, as noted above.)

Dwyer also noted that on numerous occasions throughout the events leading up to the trial and during the trial, there were "leaks" from the Justice Department to the press. Dwyer noted that it is generally a crime for a prosecutor to leak grand jury information, but that few have ever been prosecuted for such a crime since it would require prosecutors to investigate themselves.

In his final statement Dwyer also charged the Justice Department with abuse of process by using extra-legal tactics in order to obtain evidence against him. In one instance, U.S. Attorney West and a FBI agent told a state Treasury Department employee that they had evidence that William Smith had offered to pay off the employee's mortgage if he helped them get the CTA contract approved.

The only problem was this: The Treasury Department employee was a renter and never had a mortgage to begin with. Furthermore, according to Dwyer, the Treasury Department employee had been subpoenaed to appear before the grand jury, but the grand jury wasn't even in session that day. It was a ruse, Dwyer said, by the Justice Department to bring the employee in for questioning.

Dwyer also took particular issue with West's use of plea bargaining, especially with Torquato, in setting up the case against him. Torquato's sentence was reduced considerably, and after he was actually sent to prison, West lobbied successfully with the U.S. Parole Commission for a further reduction in the sentence.

Dwyer said that what West did was "virtually unheard of." Dwyer contended that: "Normally, when a prosecutor appears before a parole board, it is to urge that a felon serve [his] full term."

In response to Dwyer's charges, West said he denied both Smith and Torquato immunity from prosecution when they agreed to give testimony about Dwyer's role in the case. "And that's highly unusual in a bribery case," he added.

"Usually," said West, "when a participant in a bribery case (either the person who offered the bribe or the person who accepted the bribe) offers to give testimony in return for immunity, it is often granted. But not in this case.

"When Smith and Torquato approached us with the

request for immunity, we said, 'No deal, folks.'"

According to West, the FBI had already accumulated enough evidence to readily convict the two men. "I didn't feel that it was necessary or appropriate to offer them immunity under the circumstances," said West.

West acknowledged that he did indeed intervene with the U.S. Parole Commission on behalf of Torquato, urging that his sentence be reduced: "When anyone cooperates with the government in an investigation," he said, "we are required to bring that cooperation to the attention of the court and the parole board and that is exactly what I did."

Of Dwyer's final statement, West claimed: "It slants everything completely."

West claimed that he forwarded a copy of Dwyer's statement to the Justice Department, noting in another interview that while he certainly didn't agree with the substance of Dwyer's charges against him, "Somebody should review them and ask whatever questions need to be asked."

At the time, according to a Justice Department spokesman, John Russell, "a very preliminary review" of the case was being conducted by the department's Office of Professional Responsibility. Russell, said, however, that with Dwyer dead, he doubts the inquiry will get into what he called "an investigative stage" in which FBI agents would have to conduct personal interviews with everyone involved in the case.

Critics have suggested that an in-house Justice Department investigation of its own activities would be a farce. There was even some question at this point as to whether or not it was West's referral (of Dwyer's complaint) that sparked the investigation to begin with.

Initially, Russell of the Justice Department announced that an investigation had been requested by Sen. Joe Biden (D-Del.), chairman of the Senate Judiciary Committee, and by Sen. Edward M. Kennedy (D-Mass.). But a judiciary committee spokeswoman denied that the senators had anything to do with the request. Sometime later Russell announced that he had been mistaken and that it was West's own efforts that launched the in-house inquiry.

Dwyer's defenders, of whom there were many, suggested that the only objective official inquiry could come through the egis of Congress. But Dwyer hoped that the media would use its power to push Congress into launching an investigation of his case.

In his final statement, Dwyer told the press: "To those of you who are shallow, the events of this morning will be that story. But to those of you with depth and concern the real story will be what I hope and pray results from this morning: in the coming months and years the development of a true justice system here in the United States."

Quoting muckraking journalist Lincoln Steffans, Dwyer final statement concluded (sadly): "I am going to die in office in an effort to see if the shameful facts, spread out in all their shame, will not burn through our civic shamelessness and set fire to American pride."

He begged the media: "Please tell my story on every radio and television station and in every newspaper and magazine in the United States."

The story of Dwyer's suicide was indeed told—around the world. But not the full story.

Dwyer's wife, Joann, later told *The Spotlight* that "The stories that appeared in the media did not correspond with what I heard in the courtroom."

For example, she said, "If you go over the court records, you'll see that none of the witnesses ever even said he accepted a bribe. I can remember Budd saying that after (and not before) the contract was signed—and this came out in court—they approached him about making contributions to his re-election campaign, that they wanted to throw a fund-raiser on his behalf.

"But Budd said:'No way. I don't want anything to do with that. I don't want anything to do with any of you who had anything to do with this contract because I did not exchange the contract in return for any money or any contributions.' That also came out in the trial."

Mrs. Dwyer also outlined to *The Spotlight* how one of the key prosecution witnesses against her husband, William Smith, had changed his story:

> Unfortunately, I feel that when Mr. Smith eventually changed his story and testified against Budd he was very, very convincing. As a matter of fact I found myself crying at his testimony where he said, "I would do anything to save my wife," and he broke down and cried. I felt the tears coming down, and I thought, "Here I am crying for someone who is trying to put my husband in jail."
>
> I had such a deep interest in my own husband, yet I felt such sympathy for that man. So I can imagine how the jury must have felt.
>
> Budd had even been a defense witness for Mr. Smith whe he was on trial. And my husband told the truth for Mr. Smith. Under the intervening circumstances, what could Mr. Smith have done?
>
> In the period between Smith's trial and my husband's trial, the U.S. attorney's office promised Smith his sentence would be reduced and that his wife would not also be indicted and go to jail (because they thought that she had something to do with the conspiracy) if he changed his story and testified against Budd.
>
> They said to Smith, "We need this testimony, or your children will be orphans."
>
> If the man had a choice between Budd Dwyer and his own family, who was he going to choose?

Although it was not publicly revealed until the day after his death, Dwyer (as noted earlier) had rejected a plea bargain that would have resulted in a five-year prison sentence instead of the potential 55-year sentence and an accompanying massive fine. Dwyer simply and absolutely refused to plead guilty to a crime he did not commit.

According to Mrs. Dwyer, "Budd said: 'How can I plea bargain the truth? What do I have to plea bargain with?' He said: 'I can't lie. There's nothing to plea bargain with. I've told the truth.' Budd said, 'I'll spend 20 years in prison before I'll lie.'"

Mrs Dwyer, remarkably, reflected no bitterness about the tragedy that befell her husband and her family. "That was thanks to Budd," she said, adding:

> I used to be a much more vindictive person, unlike my husband. And that's one thing Budd asked of me in the letter he left me. He said: "JoAnn, get rid of the bitterness. Do not be vindictive. You waste your energies.
>
> "Make a positive effort against the system—not against people," he said. "Their consciences will take care of them. They will be taken care of in good time." And there's one thing else he said, and that's "On Judgment Day there'll be no plea bargaining."
>
> It will all come out eventually.

When asked if her husband was a proverbial "good guy in a bad business," Mrs. Dwyer responded:

> Too good of a guy in a bad business. He gave us so much to live for. We feel so fortunate.
>
> For me to have had that type of a person for 23 years, as much as I miss him, and we had some bad times, and I know that some of them are going to be worse, I don't know who else could have been so happy as I've been.

I have a sign in my bedroom. It says "One Day at a Time." I'm going to do everything I can to vindicate my husband. I've received over 3,000 letters—99 percent of them say:"Your husband was an innocent man." A lot of them start out with "You don't know me, but. . ." and they want to tell me about something Budd has done for them or how he helped them.

I think that my dedication to Budd and everything that he has given me to live for is going to be a very sustaining factor in my life.

My biggest fear is that after what happened to Budd, as good and honest and decent a man as ever became involved in politics, good people might not want to get involved in politics if they have to go through this kind of thing.

It is a very, very scary thing to happen in America. I'm thinking of the general public and what can happen to the average person.

I received a letter from one lady whose son was incarcerated and she is sure he is innocent.

Who is going to listen to these people? Somebody has to listen to these people. It's not just, as my husband called it, "big pelts" who suffer, it's also, as we've always considered ourselves, the common everyday person who is in jeopardy.

It can happen to anyone.

Budd loved life. He worked 23 years for the very system that betrayed him and he could not believe it was all actually happening. For the last few months, he constantly said to me:"JoAnn, if it can happen to us, how many other people has it happened to?"

Budd was a wonderful, wonderful, honest man. I think, unfortunately, that wonderful sense of honesty may have been his greatest fault.

Budd was brought up by very religious parents.

We had a great thought that our lives were often being directed. We talked about this so often.

There was no reason for a very shy—and he was very shy when he started—24-year-old from Blooming Valley, Pennsylvania to someday become state treasurer with no political legacy, no money in the family—just hard work and people's love.

He was understanding, and I would say that if he had one fault it was that he trusted everyone. I didn't all the time and he'd say, "JoAnn, how can you make a judgment like that?"

He trusted everyone, until they betrayed him.

Budd could not believe that this could happen in the United States—the things that we went through during those 30 months.

But he was not a "confused" or "paranoiac" individual, as former Gov. Thornburgh's press secretary alleged in a public statement. He was very much in control of what he thought and what he did.

Mrs. Dwyer actually described her husband's suicide as "the greatest act of love that I have ever seen." She said:

He loved us so much and we had such a great life together that I know what he did was an act of love. It was not an act of selfishness. The same media that helped persecute him can also help correct the system. And Budd had to get to that media.

He wanted nobody else in that room (when he committed suicide) at the time, except the media. He tried to get the entire staff, anyone he loved, out of that room. That's why he put such a heavy burden on the media. And I said, "good."

I'm so glad he did. Where was the media when we were trying to explain our side of the story?

Now the media has that heavy burden. Now it's up to the media to take the ball and carry it, and do something about it.

Unfortunately, the media did *not* take the ball and carry it. Instead, in the weeks following Dwyer's death and the distribution of his final statement, the Establishment media energetically did its best to smother the charges made by Dwyer regarding the manner in which former Pennsylvania Gov. Dick Thornburgh used his influence in Justice Department circles to engineer Dwyer's conviction.

Thornburgh himself issued a comment, through a spokesman, to the effect that he would have "no statement" regarding Dwyer's charges, although Thornburgh's former press secretary David Runkel was quoted as saying that Dwyer's charges were "confused" and "paranoic."

Now the Associated Press (AP), in a story published in newspapers throughout the state of Pennsylvania, actively sought to clear Thornburgh's name.

One dispatch, published in the *Erie Sunday Times*, was headlined "Dwyer's Assertions Unproven: Even His Close Friends Reject any Thornburgh Conspiracy."

The story, by AP writer David Morris, stated flatly that "evidence never made public . . . appears to support a federal jury's finding that Dwyer conspired to accept bribes in return for awarding a lucrative contract to [Computer Technology Associates (CTA)]."

(It was AP writer Morris who wrote the newswire's nationally distributed "news" dispatch, which proclaimed that Dwyer had read a "rambling" statement to the press before he committed suicide. As *The Spotlight* demonstrated to its readers, there was absolutely nothing "rambling" about the statement in any way, shape or form.)

The evidence upon which AP made its claim was an unpublished interview that the *Philadelphia Daily News* conducted with William T. Smith, a representative of the company, CTA, that allegedly offered a bribe to Dwyer.

The interview, conducted five days after Smith was indicted for his role in the affair, reportedly included Smith's statement that he offered Dwyer a bribe and that Dwyer had agreed to accept the bribe.

As noted earlier, Smith initially pleaded not guilty on charges of having offered Dwyer a bribe. However, after his conviction, Smith agreed to change his story, "admit" that he had previously given false testimony, and hen testify against Dwyer in return for a promise by the acting U.S. attorney who was prosecuting the case, James West, that West would not ask for an indictment against Smith's wife. West further agreed to support Smith's bid for a reduced sentence, which Smith had, by that point, now formally requested.

The AP story never once noted that Dwyer, in his final statement, revealed that Smith had told him that he (Smith) had not, in fact, offered Dwyer a bribe, but that, instead, he had only told his superior at CTA, John Torquato, that he had offered Dwyer a bribe.

Before changing his story, Smith had said that Torquato insisted that he, Smith, offer a bribe to Dwyer, which Smith did not want to do. Nor, said Smith, did he believe a bribe was necessary in order to get Dwyer's approval of the state treasury's pending contract with CTA.

As evidence that Smith offered Dwyer a bribe the AP story stated: "Government records show Smith refused a polygraph test in August, 1984, after he told FBI agents he did not make or promise campaign contributions to any Republican or Democratic Committee, any state official or state employee."

The AP's "evidence" in this regard was suspect, to say the least, in light of the fact that it was common knowledge that Smith and Torquato admitted to having offered bribes to individuals other than Dwyer.

That Smith might, five days after his indictment, have told *The Philadelphia Daily News* that he had offered Dwyer a bribe is quite possible.

However, as Dwyer himself noted in his final statement: "Both Smith and Torquato knew they had legal problems for bribing Dave Herbert [the former Pennsylvania state director of Social Security for public employees] to provide false and incomplete information to [the Treasury Department task force reviewing the pending CTA contract].

"Smith knew from his limited criminal law practice and Torquato learned from his attorney [according to their testimony] that U.S. attorneys and FBI agents are interested in 'big pelts'."

Thus Smith, after his indictment, may have initially determined that his best strategy would be to accuse Dwyer of complicity in order to ultimately bargain for a reduced sentence for himself if his forthcoming trial went against him.

Again, from Dwyer's statement: "Bill Smith was slick ... He not only went to two attorneys with his 'offer of proof' but I understand he also told at least one member of the capital press corps in the event his trial went badly and he needed additional prior verification of his story to work out a future deal." That is what Smith was now doing, with the apparent collaboration and support of the AP.

The AP was obviously determined to clear former Gov. Dick Thornburgh of Dwyer's allegation that the then-governor was out to "get" him and that he used the CTA investigation as the means to do so.

Citing statements by two of Dwyer's Treasury Department employees, whom the AP called "close friends" of Dwyer, the AP dismissed Dwyer's charges against Thornburgh. The AP quoted one employee as saying: "I never thought Dick Thornburgh personally tried to engineer the whole scenario."

Yet, as the AP failed to note, Dwyer never alleged that

Thornburgh had personally tried to engineer the entire case. Dwyer only stated that when the CTA investigation was under way (spurred on by a Democratic state official, state Auditor General Al Benedict, who was Dwyer's unsuccessful re-election opponent in 1984), Thornburgh encouraged the investigation, which was being conducted by Thornburgh's two-time appointee, acting U.S. Attorney West.

The AP also suggested that somehow it was Dwyer's fault that he became involved with John Torquato since Dweyr knew that Torquato's father, a longtime Democratic Party political boss, had been sent to prison on extortion charges some years before.

However, as Mrs. Dwyer told *The Spotlight*: "Budd had [the younger] Torquato thoroughly checked out before he agreed to have any dealings with him. All the evidence indicated that Torquato was clean.

"He'd had some business dealings with some major corporations, for example, and no problems were evident there. Budd didn't believe in holding the son responsible for the sins of the father."

This, of course, was Dwyer's honest mistake, but the AP would have had its readers believe that Dwyer's dealings with Torquato and CTA were somehow, in their genesis, unworthy.

Clearly, the AP and the Establishment media were determined to bury the Dwyer case from public inspection. But in order to do so, the AP was distorting the truth.

Ultimately, *The Spotlight*'s stories about Budd Dwyer were widely circulated throughout Pennsylvania by friends and admirers of the late treasurer and word soon spread, particularly within Republican Party ranks, of the behind-the-scenes treachery that led to Dwyer's frame-up and subsequent conviction leading to his tragic death.

Former Governor Dick Thornburgh went on to serve as attorney general in the administrations of Ronald Reagan and George H. W. Bush. Then, in 1991, Thornburgh resigned from the cabinet to run for the U.S. Senate as the Republican candidate to succeed the late Sen. John Heinz, who had died in an airplane crash.

Although the media in Pennsylvania and across the country (which was obviously "Thornburgh-Friendly") widely predicted a thoroughgoing victory for Thornburgh—who acted throughout the campaign as though he had already been elected—the voters of Pennsylvania had a surprise for Thornburgh and the media: Democratic candidate Harris Wofford defeated Thornburgh in a massive upset victory that embarrassed Thornburgh's media promoters (and Thornburgh himself).

The fact was that many Pennsylvania Republicans had long memories and held Thornburgh's intrigues against Budd Dwyer against their Senate candidate and chose either to vote against him or simply stay home. The Budd Dwyer Affair was the real reason Thornburgh was defeated, but, predictably, the mass media chose not to say so.

Unfortunately, of course, Budd Dwyer was just one of many innocent victims of high-level corruption in the Justice Department and many more were to come—including Jim Traficant.

The big question is how many more people will suffer at the hands of the Justice Department in the future.

More "Must-Read" Best-Sellers
By America's No-Holds-Barred
Author, Lecturer &
Radio Talk Show Host
MICHAEL COLLINS PIPER

THE GOLEM:
ISRAEL'S NUCLEAR HELL BOMB AND THE ROAD TO GLOBAL ARMAGEDDON

The Case for Dismantling Our Planet's Most Dangerous Arsenal of Atomaic Weapons of Mass Destruction

BY MICHAEL COLLINS PIPER

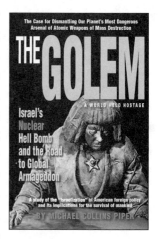

In this landmark work, the author pulls no punches in asserting that Israel's nuclear Hell Bomb—which Piper has dubbed "The Golem" —is pushing civilization toward global Armageddon, that the perpetuation of this un-controlled weapons program has left the world held hostage. Piper explains the danger the planet faces as a consequence of American collaboration with a nuclear-armed Israel, a nation which has an open historical record of hostility to other peoples, based on little-known Jewish religious teachings that have been the philosophy upon which Israel—since its earliest days—has worked relentlessly to construct an atomic arsenal, the very foundation of its national security strategy. This is the book that also, unswervingly, takes on what Piper calls "the Israelization of American foreign policy." This is the book that explains the nature of the forces now demanding war with Iran, just as they got us into Iraq.. *The Golem*, **softcover, 198 pages, $25 per copy.**

Order from FIRST AMENDMENT BOOKS, 645 Pennsylvania Avenue SE, Suite 100, Washington, D.C. 20003. No charge for shipping & handling inside the United States. Call 1-888-699-NEWS (6397) toll free to charge to Visa or MasterCard.

THE JUDAS GOATS:
THE ENEMY WITHIN

The Shocking Never-Before-Told Story
of the Infiltration and Subversion
of the American Nationalist Movement

BY MICHAEL COLLINS PIPER

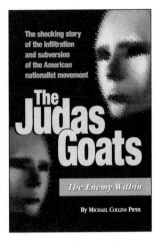

This amazing volume demonstrates how, during the course of the 20th century, paid agents and disrupters, working on behalf of the Zionist cause and for the international interests of the Rothschild banking empire, infiltrated and subverted American nationalist groups. Here is a detailed overview of the intrigues of the infamous Anti-Defamation League of B'nai B'rith, the corruption of the FBI and the CIA by Zionist elements, the evidence pointing toward Israeli involvement in the Oklahoma City bombing, the strange, little-known story of how Trotskyite elements seized command of the American "conservative" movement and also played a role in manipulating Sen. Joseph R. McCarthy's hunt for communists in high places, a study of the secret powers behind Rupert Murdoch's media empire and much, much more. Guaranteed: You won't be able to put this stunning book down. *The Judas Goats,* **softcover, 376 pages, $25 per copy.**

Order from FIRST AMENDMENT BOOKS, 645 Pennsylvania Avenue SE, Suite 100, Washington, D.C. 20003. No charge for shipping & handling inside the United States. Call 1-888-699-NEWS (6397) toll free to charge to Visa or MasterCard.

Zionist Influence on the American Media
Michael Collins Piper's Historic Address to the Arab League

On March 10, 2003, Michael Collins Piper sparked a firestorm of frenzy from the Zionist lobby in America, when he addressed the topic of "Zionist Influence on the American Media." Piper was the featured speaker at the Arab League's official think tank, the distinguished Zayed Centre for Coordination and Follow-Up based in Abu Dhabi in the United Arab Emirates. Here's the un-censored text of Piper's historic speech—the first ever in more than fifty years by an American nationalist to an official assembly of the Arab League. Read for yourself what journalists, ambassadors and opinion-makers from around the globe heard in Abu Dhabi. Piper upset the Zionists for daring to say who really controls the media in America and how they have used that power to shape the course of American and world affairs. There is no copyright on this document. This 8.5 x 11 document is yours to reproduce at your own expense for widespread distribution. This is a fast-moving and interesting overview of a complex and controversial topic, but one which addresses the issue in an honest and well-documented fashion. You'll be pleased to pass on copies to friends and associates who need to learn the facts about this political phenomenon. *Zionist Influence on the American Media*, softcover, Six two-sided pages (numbered 1-12). Donation: $10.

Order from First Amendment Books, 645 Pennsylvania Avenue SE, Suite 100, Washington, D.C. 20003. No charge for shipping & handling inside the United States. Call 1-888-699-NEWS (6397) toll free to charge to Visa or MasterCard.

THE NEW JERUSALEM
Zionist Power in America

By Michael Collins Piper

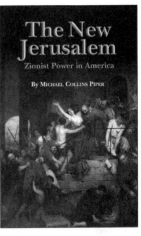

Unlike anything ever published in the modern day, this explosive study combines in 184 pages—for the first time ever between two covers—all of the amazing facts and figures which document the massive accumulation of wealth and power by those who have used that influence to direct the course of U.S. foreign and domestic policy today. And what makes this volume all the more valuable is the fact that it is based on the work of Jewish sources and Jewish authors—not the rantings of "anti-Semites" or "hatemongers." While there are many historical books on "the Israeli lobby" and about Zionist intrigues, etc, this is the only book that brings things "up to date" and constitutes a bold and thorough inquiry. Chapters include a list of prominent figures throughout history accused of "anti-Zionism" and "anti-Semitism," a detailed dissection of the Bronfman family, who are often called "the Royal family of American Zionism," an eye-opening summary of some 200 little-known, immensely wealthy Zionist families in America; a fascinating inquiry in to the infamous Enron and INSLAW affairs, documenting the suppressed "Zionist connection" plus more. Once again, *The New Jerusalem*, softcover, 176 pages, $20.

THE *HIGH PRIESTS* OF *WAR*

The Secret History of How America's Neo-Conservative Trotskyites Came to Power and Orchestrated the War in Iraq as the First Step in Their Drive for Global Empire

BY MICHAEL COLLINS PIPER

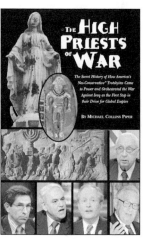

The all-time first-ever history of how America's "neo-conservative" Trotskyites came to power and orchestrated the war against Iraq as a primary step in the drive for Global Empire, the so-called New World Order. Although since this book was first published there have been many books released about the neo-cons, but this still remains the only one that tells the entire story—no holds-barred. A fast-moving narrative that's a great book to give friends and associates for a better understanding of the forces misdirecting American foreign policy. The book is being circulated internationally and translated into Japanese, Malay and Arabic, acclaimed as the one book that explains the "who, what, when, where, why and how" of the tragic involvement of the United States in the Iraq war. This fast-paced, carefully-documented 144-page volume has helped spread the word about the REAL reason for the Iraq war and how it is all part of a grand design that is being suppressed by the Controlled Media. Large photo section shows who these neo-cons are and the role they play in the plot. *The High Priests of War*, softcover, 144 pages, $20.

Order from FIRST AMENDMENT BOOKS, 645 Pennsylvania Avenue SE, Suite 100, Washington, D.C. 20003. No charge for shipping & handling inside the United States. Call 1-888-699-NEWS (6397) toll free to charge to Visa or MasterCard.

DIRTY SECRETS

Crime, Conspiracy & Cover-Up in the 20th Century

Based on the Writings and Interviews of Michael Collins Piper
Compiled and Edited by Victor Thorn & Lisa Guliani

Mordechai Vanunu, the man who blew the whistle on Israel's illegal nuclear weapons program and served 18 years in an Israeli prison for doing so, has called Michael Collins Piper one of the most "brave and honest" journalists writing today. And now, at long last, "the best of" Michael Collins Piper has been gathered together in one place! This collection includes essays not found on the Internet, previously unpublished writings, interviews (including the long-lost *Final Judgment* tapes), reviews and insights into the JFK assassination, the Oklahoma City bombing, the Federal Reserve, FDR and Pearl Harbor, Israel's deliberate attack on the *USS Liberty*, Israel and Islamic fundamentalism, the murder of Martin Luther King, the Holocaust (from the point of view of Piper, who is of American Indian descent) and much, much more. There's a broad range of material here, certainly some of the best writing in the "alternative" press today.

Besides the essays by Piper and the transcripts of the interviews with Piper by Victor Thorn and Lisa Guliani, this book also includes synopses of three of Piper's major works—*Final Judgment, The High Priests of War* and *The New Jerusalem*. *Dirty Secrets*, softcover, 250 pages, $22.

Order from FIRST AMENDMENT BOOKS, 645 Pennsylvania Avenue SE, Suite 100, Washington, D.C. 20003. No charge for shipping & handling inside the United States. Call 1-888-699-NEWS (6397) toll free to charge to Visa or MasterCard.

FINAL JUDGMENT

The Missing Link in the JFK Assassination Conspiracy

BY MICHAEL COLLINS PIPER *(presently out of print)*

This massive 768-page volume is back from the printer in the second printing of its Sixth Edition, containing explosive new material. Some 50,000 copies of previous editions are in circulation here and around the world, documenting that JFK's obstinate efforts to prevent Israel from building nuclear weapons played a key role in the conspiracy behind JFK's assassination.

Yes, the CIA and organized crime were involved in the JFK conspiracy, but the role of Israel's intelligence agency, the Mossad, was the long-suppressed "missing link" finally unveiled in this titanic work.

Includes an extensive photo section and fascinating charts outlining the thesis. You will be amazed at what you learn in these pages. No serious critic has yet to refute this book in any way, shape or form.

Definitively the last word on the subject, endorsed by former high ranking State Department and Pentagon officials and by countless numbers of independent analysts who agree with famed JFK assassination researcher Penn Jones who said that the realm of Israeli involvement in the JFK affair was a topic that needed to be explored.

GUARANTEED: You'll never look at the JFK assassination—or the events of the last half of the 20th century—in the same way again *Final Judgment*, softcover, 768 pages, 1,000+ footnotes, $25.

Order from FIRST AMENDMENT BOOKS, 645 Pennsylvania Avenue SE, Suite 100, Washington, D.C. 20003. No charge for shipping & handling inside the United States. Call 1-888-699-NEWS (6397) toll free to charge to Visa or MasterCard.

Here's what some big names have said about Michael Collins Piper's underground best-seller, *Final Judgment—The Missing Link in the JFK Assassination Conspiracy*:

"As one who has read over 200 books on the JFK assassination, and engaged in research both as an individual and as part of various teams, I can say without fear of contradiction that Piper's book is now the definitive work on the JFK assassination. *Final Judgment* is the most thorough, most honest, most penetrating, most factual, and most analytically complete and systematic of all that I have read so far. Michael Collins Piper has struck gold. JFK assassination research has a new standard bearer. It will never be the same again. *Final Judgment* is a masterpiece."

—HERBERT L. CALHOUN, PH.D.

(Dr. Calhoun retired as deputy division chief of the Policy, Plans and Analysis Office of the State Department's Bureau of Political-Military Affairs and formerly served as a senior foreign affairs specialist for the U.S. Arms Control and Disarmament Agency.)

* * *

"I think you've pinned the tail on the donkey. In my estimation, Final Judgment ranks as the most important book of the 20th century."

—WILLIAM J. GILL

(The former executive director of the Allegheny Foundation and author of such books as *Trade Wars Against America*, *The Ordeal of Otto Otepka*, and *Why Reagan Won*, Gill was a journalist with UPI and the *Pittsburgh Press* and also wrote for *Life, Fortune, The Saturday Evening Post, Reader's Digest* and *National Geographic*.)

* * *

Here's what Colonel Donn de Grand Pré has written in his own book, *Barbarians Inside the Gates*, citing *Final Judgment*, which Grand Pré describes as "brilliant". . .

"Several high-level military officers believed that the killing of JFK was in fact a coup d'etat carried out by elements of the CIA working with the Israeli Mossad. Kennedy was attempting to halt the development of nuclear weapons by the Israelis, while simultaneously planning to disband the CIA and disengage our military troops from the Indo-China area. (Read *Final Judgment* by Michael Collins Piper for more details.)"

—COL. DONN DE GRAND PRÉ

* * *

(In 1967 Grand Pré was named Director for Ground Weapons Systems in the Pentagon's Office of International Logistics Negotiations, responsible for negotiating sales contracts with heads of foreign nations for military weapons systems. On Sept. 30, 1979, *The Washington Post Magazine* wrote of Grand Pré: "If you had been a Middle Eastern ruler in the 1970s in search of American weapons systems, you would have called Donn de Grand Pré, Pentagon arms peddler.")

FINAL JUDGMENT—the one book that, if read by enough people, will turn American politics upside down . . .

A gutsy newspaper with some powerful enemies . . .

A no-nonsense independent weekly alternative to the "processed news" of the corporate Media Monopoly.

The one news outlet that dared to publish this book!

American Free Press (AFP) is the maverick national media voice that's been in the forefront reporting the uncensored news that the Controlled Media in America either ignores or suppresses.

You can count on AFP to bring the news that the major media either can not or will not report. Employee-owned-and-operated with no partisan axes to grind, AFP's reporters are committed to the truth, no matter whose ox gets gored.

AFP is the one national newspaper that's dared to tackle the Israeli lobby head on and challenge that clique of neo-conservative warmongers—that well-financed ring of arms dealers, lobbyists and "ex-Trotskyites"—who forced America into the no-win debacle in Iraq. AFP brings its readers the important stories consigned to the Orwellian Memory Hole by the self-styled "mainstream" media.

Each week—20 pages of uncensored news and information on a wide variety of topics, ranging from civil liberties and the fight against the police state to alternative health and wholistic therapies, taxes and finance, trade and foreign policy. You name it. AFP is on the cutting edge.

Big-name political figures and a host of powerful special interest groups have worked overtime to silence AFP's unswerving journalists whose track record is one that's unmatched by any other independent media voice today. If you have any doubts, why not take a look at AFP for yourself.

Isn't it time you subscribe?

American Free Press: $59 for ONE year (weekly issues) OR try out a 16-week introductory subscription for only $17.76.

Call 1-888-699-NEWS (6397) today and charge a subscription to Visa or MasterCard.

Send your check, money order or credit card information (including expiration date) to:

American Free Press
645 Pennsylvania Avenue SE, Suite 100
Washington, D.C. 20003

Check us out at www.americanfreepress.net
Online Subscriptions Also Available!

A LETTER FROM THE AUTHOR . . .

MICHAEL COLLINS PIPER
P.O. BOX 15728
WASHINGTON, DC 20003
EMAIL: PIPERM2@LYCOS.COM

Dear Reader:

The story of what happened to Jim Traficant (and before him, Budd Dwyer) is a lesson for all of us. We need to understand that "our" justice system has been taken over, corrupted, made the tool of powerful forces determined to silence any and all who would dare to challenge the powers-that-be.

But Jim Traficant and Budd Dwyer are hardly the first—and certainly (sadly) will not be the last—victims of this horrific conspiracy . . . and "conspiracy" is quite correctly the term to describe it.

We need to stand united in opposition to those who are destroying our country and destroying those public figures who have stood in their path.

And we need to make sure that, in the future, we get leaders in office---real leaders---who are ready to challenge the status quo, prepared to take on the big battles that must be fought to restore America.

On a personal note, I appreciate the encouragement of my readers and their constructive criticism of my work. I could not continue without this support.

Best Wishes and God Bless You!

Mike

MICHAEL COLLINS PIPER